LE
VIN A LA MAISON

ALL ABOUT FRENCH WINE

LE
VIN A LA MAISON

ALL ABOUT FRENCH WINE

Louis Plessis

WARD LOCK LIMITED · LONDON

Le Vin à la Maison
© Flammarion 1979
English translation and adaptation
© Ward Lock Limited 1985

First published in English in Great Britain in 1985
by Ward Lock Limited, 82 Gower Street,
London WC1E 6EQ, an Egmont Company.

Designed by Melissa Orrom
Illustrations by G. J. Galswothy

Text filmset in Garamond
by Fakenham Photosetting Limited,
Fakenham, Norfolk

Printed and bound in Spain by
Graficromo, S.A., Cordoba

British Library Cataloguing in Publication Data

Plessis, Louis
    Le vin a la maison : all about French wine.
    1. Wine and wine making – France
    I. Title
    641.2′2′0944   TP553

    ISBN 0–7063–6400–7

Translated by Anne Parry in association with First Edition

CONTENTS

FOREWORD 8

PART I
1 CLASSIFICATION AND IDENTIFICATION OF WINE 10
2 THE CHOICE OF WINES 15
3 SERVING WINE 23
4 TALKING ABOUT WINE 28
5 STORING WINE 32
6 WHAT IS WINE? 36

PART II
7 BORDEAUX 46
8 DORDOGNE 60
9 THE SOUTHWEST AND THE PYRENEES 62
10 LES CHARENTES 67
11 BURGUNDY 70
12 MÂCONNAIS, BEAUJOLAIS, LYONNAIS 83
13 THE CÔTES DU RHÔNE 89
14 PROVENCE, LANGUEDOC, CORSICA 94
15 CENTRAL PLATEAU, BOURBONNAIS, BERRY-
   NIVERNAIS 106
16 THE LOIRE VALLEY 112
17 CHAMPAGNE 121
18 LORRAINE, ALSACE 127
19 JURA, THE ALPS 132
20 SPIRITS 137

FOREWORD

French cuisine may be the best in the world, and France may produce the finest wines in the world. But it is remarkable how rarely one finds a combination of excellence – even in France itself.

How is it that famous restaurants are only able to produce wine lists of colourless mediocrity? Why, in a province that is famed for its cooking, is it so difficult to find a bottle that is worthy of accompanying the food which a talented chef, with all his artistry, can produce?

The high price of a good bottle of wine, which can, unfortunately, double the cost of a meal, is probably the main cause of this sad state of affairs. But there is another explanation. The role played by wine is very often a humble one: it serves only to dress up a dinner, or is used as a mere backdrop with no more importance than the tablecloth, or the flowers; it is taken for granted as part and parcel of the meal, an accessory, like the bread, oil or mustard.

The princes of olden days viewed it differently, and the cup-bearer was held in high esteem in their courts.

The present lack of regard for wine is a cause for concern. What *cordon bleu* chef has not been thrown into confusion trying to decide what should be served with a certain seafood, with a particular *gratin* or with a *feuilleté*? And how he should serve it.

Such a chef will do one of two things. He will either invent a disastrous solution, or opt out in a cowardly fashion. For example, he might produce a shabby little rosé to accompany his splendid dish. A hair in the soup could not be more effective in dampening enthusiasm for the meal.

This book attempts to help those who know that 'to invite someone as a guest is to be responsible for their happiness for as long as they are under your roof' (Brillat-Savarin). It aims to be a handbook rather than an encyclopedia, it is for those who care little that 61 Médocs were officially classed by the courtiers of Bordeaux in 1885, or that true Chablis is produced exclusively on the Kimmeridgian stage of the Upper Jurassic, or that the area of Clos Vougeot is 50 hectares and 22 acres. The book aims simply to ensure that every meal is a harmonious celebration.

PART
I

1
CLASSIFICATION AND IDENTIFICATION OF WINE

THE HIERARCHY

It is important to have a clear picture of the sacrosanct official classification. The making and labelling of wines is subject to E.E.C. wine laws.

In the language of the E.E.C. the following categories have been defined.

- *Vins de qualité produits dans des régions determinées* (V.Q.P.R.D.), quality wines produced from grapes from specified areas

- *Vins de table*, table wines.

V.Q.P.R.D. are divided into two sub-categories:

- *Vins d'appellation d'origine contrôlée* (A.O.C.)
These wines are as kings in the hierarchy; but among them are to be found blue-blooded princes as well as the insignificant marquis.

They are defined by decrees that are precise, yet always changing, specifying the grape-growing region, sometimes down to the exact parcel of land, their minimum alcohol content, their maximum yield per hectare, the minimum age of the vines, the types of grapes that may be used, the permitted height of the vines, the bottling of the wine, and so on.

- *Vins delimités de qualité supérieure* (V.D.Q.S.)
These are defined as precisely as the A.O.C. wines but occupy an inferior place in the hierarchy.

Vins de table also comprise two sub-categories:

- *Vins de pays*
These are middle-class wines, but nevertheless are obliged to guarantee departmental or regional origins, minimum alcohol content, grape types used in their production, maximum yield per hectare, and precise levels of acidity and sulphur dioxide content. They must be approved by local commissions.

- *Vins de consommation courante* (V.C.C.), wine for current consumption
This is the wine of the people, but is not without its subtleties, its character, its different moods; and it too has its stringent regulations. These are the

only wines allowed to marry, that is to be blended, but only with another wine from the E.E.C. When this is done, it is sold as *vin de coupage* (blended wine) but it really does not deserve the contempt that people are inclined to give it. A V.C.C. wine very rarely has all the qualities necessary to be totally seductive, so its joining together with a richer or more elegant wine can only add to its charm. It all depends on who conducts the marriage.

Imported wines which are not made in the E.E.C. fall outside this classification and may not be blended with French wines.

THE BOTTLE

Only glass is worthy of a quality wine. Everyday wines are increasingly being sold in boxes (plastic) and even tins; so far it has been found that these materials are only suitable for quick consumption.

Bottles vary in shape, colour and weight, dark coloured glass offering better protection from premature ageing.

The litre bottle	contains 100 centilitres
The Bordeaux-type bottle	contains 70 or 75 centilitres
The Burgundy-type bottle	contains 70 or 75 centilitres
The Alsace flute	contains 70 or 72 centilitres
The Arbois clavelin	contains 65 centilitres
The Champagne bottle	contains 80 centilitres
The port bottle	contains 75 centilitres

There are many types of regional bottles, for example in Aix, Normandy, Basques and Nantes. These are gradually being standardised to a uniform capacity of 75 centilitres. Half and quarter bottles are widespread and Bordeaux has adopted certain multiple bottles that are often copied by other vineyards:

The Magnum	contains 1.5 litres
The Double Magnum	contains 3 litres
The Jereboam	contains 5 litres
The Imperial	contains 6 litres

Champagne, on the other hand, is a little different:

The Magnum	contains 1.6 litres
The Jereboam	contains 3.2 litres
The Methusulem	contains 6.4 litres
The Balthazar	contains 12.8 litres

Besides looking special, these larger bottles have the advantage of preserving the wine better.

All these capacities are *ras goulot* (up to the neck), that is they would be correct if it were possible to fill the bottle completely. They are called available capacities (*capacités utiles*). However, the cork takes up a certain space, and a little room must be allowed for heat expansion. The real capacity (*capacité réelle* or *nominale*) printed on the foil or on the label will be slightly different.

Bottles made to a standard specified by law are gradually being introduced. These have the real capacity engraved on the side and the available capacity on the bottom, both in centilitres.

THE LABEL

A wine must declare its origins. This is a legal requirement. The label is the wine's identity card, and it is subject to complex legislation. It spells out in precise terms facts which are both useful to the consumer and demanded by law. The information on the label must be as complete as possible. It is a good idea to examine it carefully.

A *vin de consommation courante* must have on its label:

the words *vin de table*
the real capacity of the bottle
the name and address of the bottler
the alcoholic strength, which must not be less than 8.5°, or 9.5° in France for a blended wine (*vin de coupage*).

The label may also state the potential alcoholic strength, which in the case of a sweet wine is that which would exist if all the remaining sugar had been fermented out. The only additional information permitted on the label is the colour of the wine, a trade name, the names and addresses of distributors, any distinctions awarded in competitions, and serving suggestions.

Any wine made by mixing wines from different origins within the European community must have the words 'produce of several E.E.C. countries' on its label.

A *vin de pays* is subject to the same rules, but it does not have to state its alcoholic content. However, it must specify its geographical origin, which may be the name of the department of France in which it was produced, or it may be a smaller area, or it could even be a zone which covers several departments. In addition the name of the grape used in the wine and the year of the harvest may also appear.

Quality wine produced in a specified region (*appellation d'origine contrôlée* or *vin delimité de qualité supérieure*) must specify:

its *appellation*, immediately followed by the type of wine (A.O.C. or V.D.Q.S.)
the real capacity of the bottle
the name and address of the bottler.

In addition the following may appear:

the colour of the wine
the origin of the grapes, that is the name of the locality, commune or viticultural area defined by decree
the year of the harvest
a commercial brand name

the names and addresses of distributors
any distinctions awarded
the actual or potential alcoholic strength
serving suggestions
instructions on how to care for the wine
the type of product it is
the name of the grower
various quality control marks, especially the official classification of quality
(obligatory in the case of V.D.Q.S. wines)
a reference to the fact that the wine was bottled in the area of production.

An imported wine from a country outside the E.E.C. must in addition specify the country where it was produced, carry the word 'wine' on its label and also the name and address of the importer if the wine has been bottled outside the E.E.C.

The words, the letters and the illustrations on the labels must all conform to precise standards. The regulations are therefore complex but aim only to protect the consumer. One must, however, be careful, for legislation dealing with this topic is subject to continuous modification. Naturally enough, ancient vintages bottled before the time of community law, which came into force on 1 September 1976, are exempt from some of these regulations.

THE CORK

Cork is the only suitable material if the wine is to be kept for any length of time. A bottle that is to benefit from a certain amount of ageing – and we shall see that for the majority of vintage wines, this is imperative – must therefore be furnished with a cork that is healthy, supple and long enough to ensure that the wine will keep for as long as we expect it to.

Plastic or metallic caps or screw-tops can only be used on wines that will be drunk quickly. Never attempt to keep for a long time wines that have not been adequately corked.

An iron-branded cork is a guarantee of the growth, the name or the vintage.

In the case of Champagne there is no cause for alarm if a cork does not expand into the shape of a skirt as it pops out of the bottle. Such a cork is called a *cheville*, or plug, and is the proof of a laying-down period and therefore promises a good quality wine, provided that this period has not been *too* long.

The dreaded corked taste is due to a microscopic fungus that lives in the depths of the holes in the cork, regardless of its quality. Unfortunately it is not possible to offer full protection against this, and so it is a risk that has to be reckoned with.

Always be suspicious of bottles where wine has seeped through the cork and there is a large air space – there is a good chance that the wine will be affected.

THE CAPSULE

This contributes to the appearance of the bottle while at the same time completely hiding the cork that would otherwise be seen through the neck.

Foil or wax are the preferred materials. It is also an excellent guarantee of authenticity, and should be looked for. (If a metallic cap is a fiscal one, ie it guarantees that an indirect tax fee has to be paid, it must be capable of being broken, must carry a revenue stamp and the administrative number of the department where bottling took place, as well as the registration number of the bottler. The stamp should be green in the case of an *appellation d'origine contrôlée*, blue for all others.)

A darkening of the metal cap in contact with the cork, providing it is only slight, should give no cause for concern.

THE FALSE NECK

This is a small air space left between the cork and the surface of the wine. It must be large enough to allow for expansion so that the cork is not pushed out when the bottle is exposed to heat, yet small enough not to trap too much air inside the bottle. The liquid level must always come up to the neck of the bottle, and not just to the shoulder, except in the case of very old wines where a certain amount of evaporation is inevitable. A low level is not a sign of a wine that has been well kept.

2

THE CHOICE OF
WINES

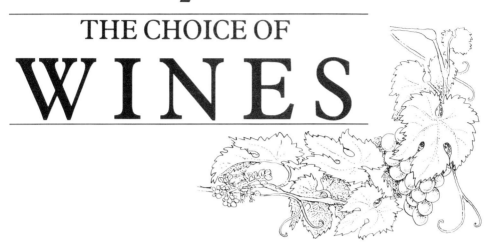

TYPES OF WINE

Red wine

Red wine comes from the fermentation of red grapes, both skin and juice remaining together with or without the stems. The colour, which comes primarily from the skins, penetrates the must in the process of crushing and fermentation.

These are nearly always dry wines, with no residual sugar, the only exception being some sweet varieties that tend not to suit the French palate and are made mostly for export.

White wine

White wine comes from white grapes or red grapes with white juice, whose skins are then separated out from the must in the preliminary pressing.

Champagne can be produced from either red or white grapes.

Blanc de blanc is made only from white grapes – literally, white wine from white grapes.

White wine may be dry or sweet, according to whether or not the wine is allowed to ferment out until all the sugar has been converted into alcohol.

Choice dessert wines, for example of the Sauternes type, come from harvests that have been partially affected by *pourriture noble*, noble rot, which concentrates the sugar. The harvesters have to go over the same bunch several times in order to pick out the single grapes at their peak. A delicate and onerous task!

Rosé wine

Rosé wine is obtained either by a preliminary pressing of dark grapes whose juice may or may not be very red before fermentation, or by rapidly drawing off the liquid from red grapes at the beginning of fermentation. In the latter case it is called a *rosé de saignée*, blood rosé.

Both dry and sweet rosés are found. Rosés are given different names according to the depth of their colour, such as *vin gris*, *vin de nuit* (this is when the grapes are harvested one day and the liquid drawn off the next), *vin de café* (this has more colour, and is mostly served in southern French cafés). The *gris de gris* comes from grapes with pale skins.

Le vin jaune (yellow wine)

This is made in the Jura, from white wine that is left for six years in casks that are never completely filled and on whose surface a thin veil of yeast develops which, by the end of the process (if it is successful), has imparted a very distinctive hazelnut flavour to the wine.

Vins de liqueur and vins doux naturels (natural sweet wines)

These are obtained by adding alcohol to a must before or during fermentation in order to maintain a high enough sugar content. The latter differ from the former only in that they must have an *appellation d'origine contrôlée*.

Sparkling wines

These contain a significant quantity of carbon dioxide which has either been simply added to them (carbonated wines) or which they have acquired in the process of secondary fermentation which takes place either in closed vats or bottles (champagne method). *Crémants* (foamy), *pétillants* (bubbly) and *perlants* (pearly) wines have less gas in them and produce a lighter sparkle.

AROMA AND BOUQUET

The smell of a wine is one of its most distinguishing characteristics, and it is important to recognise the difference between the terms 'aroma' and 'bouquet'. The aroma comes from the grape itself; it appears very early, but disappears after a relatively short time – six months to two years. It is caused by oxidation, from the air that is dissolved in the wine. It is the smell of the fruit, enriched by a secondary aroma created by the specific conditions of fermentation.

The bouquet is created by subtle combinations of volatile elements and develops only very slowly and away from the air, that is after a relatively long time in the bottle.

There are some grape varieties which typically produce an excellent aroma, such as Gamay or Beaujolais, but which are not inclined to develop a notable bouquet. Others, such as the Pinot of Burgundy or the Cabernet of Bordeaux initially have only a modest scent, but as they age develop a superb bouquet. It used to be said that the latter group aged well, but that the former came to a bad end. Aromatic wines are best drunk young, whereas wines with bouquet often need to be kept in the bottle for a long time.

Among the reds, most of the wines of the Midi, as well as Mâcon and Beaujolais, belong in the first category. They are intended to be fruity, fresh

Marks for quality given to *appellation d'origine contrôlée* wines

	BORDEAUX	RED BURGUNDY	WHITE BURGUNDY	SAUTERNES	LOIRE	RHÔNE	ALSACE
1945	10	10	8	10	9	10	9
1947	9	9	9	10	10	9	10
1948	6	6	7	7	5	8	7
1949	7	9	8	8	8	8	8
1950	5	3	5	4	6	6	6
1952	6	7	7	6	5	7	3
1953	9	8	4	9	9	5	7
1955	9	8	9	10	9	8	9
1957	6	7	7	9	8	7	5
1959	8	9	9	9	9	3	9
1960	3	0	1	3	4	5	6
1961	9	8	8	9	8	8	9
1962	5	6	7	6	7	7	7
1963	1	1	3	1	2	1	2
1964	7	8	8	2	9	7	8
1965	0	0	0	1	1	2	4
1966	8	9	9	8	5	8	7
1967	6	7	8	9	6	6	6
1968	0	0	1	3	3	5	5
1969	5	9	10	6	8	4	9
1970	9	8	8	9	6	8	8
1971	7	6	7	8	7	7	9
1972	2	6	6	5	6	6	4
1973	4	5	7	6	7	3	5
1974	4	4	2	5	8	0	6
1975	9	2	3	8	7	2	7
1976	8	9	10	8	10	6	9
1977	6	5	6	5	4	7	5
1978	8	8	9	6	7	8	8
1979*	7	8	7	7	6	9	8
1980*	5	5	6	8	6	8	6

* Marks are given subject to the wines' ageing.

and attractive. *Premiers crus*, first growths, are always wines with a bouquet – Bordeaux, Burgundy and also the red wines of the Loire (Chinon, Bourgeuil) and Châteauneuf-du-Pape.

White wines that need to be drunk young are the wines of Provence, the Muscadets, Sancerre, Pouilly Fumé, Sauvignon and Gaillac. On the other hand the great Burgundies, the Chablis from Chardonnay grapes, the Anjous from Chenin grapes, and above all the distinguished sweet Bordeaux take a long time to acquire their full bouquet.

Commercially produced champagnes and sparkling wines have nothing to gain from being kept after the initial obligatory storage time. There is little point building up a large stock of aromatic wines, but every reason to store in your cellar some wines that need to mature slowly in order to reach their most dazzling brilliance.

THE CRU (GROWTH)

This is the main factor in determining the nobility of a bottle of wine, and it is always the same estates that produce the best wines. It is a remarkable feat, and one that has been accomplished by winemakers selecting the land over the course of centuries, reserving for their vines those areas which will give the best results. As it happens, the vine often produces its best grapes on relatively poor soil, leaving the more fertile land free for more demanding crops. The round, smooth pebbles of Châteauneuf-du-Pape, the gravel of Bordeaux and the scrubland of Languedoc are all unable to produce satisfactory grain harvests or lush pastures, but the vine, with its long roots, thrives in these areas.

The site is equally important in determining how good a growth will be; the best is almost always in the extreme north of the viticultural area and often in a river valley, such as the Garonne, Loire, Rhône, Saône or Rhine. Exposure to the sun, altitude, climate and rainfall also play important roles.

Another essential ingredient is the *cépage*, the type of vine, that is grown. Great wines are always produced from a traditional *cépage* that is very well adapted to the conditions of the area. Some vineyards are only planted with one particular variety; for instance, Beaujolais with Gamay; Burgundy with Pinot in its varying forms for reds and Chardonnay for whites; and Vouvray with Chenin. Other areas are associated with several varieties such as Bordeaux with its Cabernet franc, Cabernet-Sauvignon, Merlot, Malbec and Petite Verdot for the reds and Sauvignon, Semillon and Muscadelle for the whites.

Occasionally, all these factors and others combine in such a felicitous way as to produce a *grand cru*.

THE VINTAGE

The cultivation of wine is a matter of fluctuation and balance. Too much heat makes the wine heavy, too much cold prevents the grape from attaining perfect maturity. Too little water is harmful to the foliage, too much affects the fruit. Although warm years tend to be the best, a good balance of sun and rain is more important; mild, consistent, fairly dry weather is more favourable than extremes. The weather conditions of a given year make or break a vintage.

Bottles without a year written on the label contain either *vin de consommation courante* or wines from two or more vintages that have been blended so as to avoid big differences in quality. In Champagne and a few other vineyards vintage wines are only made in good years.

Unfortunately, a really good year is very rare, and one must mistrust those enthusiasts who discover the wine of the century in every harvest.

FOOD AND WINE

The relationship between good food and good wine is a subtle one: each must do justice to the other without clashing or competing with it.

The order of service

A menu must be planned to allow for the wines to be served in a logical order. There are certain ground rules:

- White wines should be served before red wines
- Dry wines, whether red or white, should precede sweet wines
- Light wines should come before full bodied wines.

Thus, you would serve:

- White Burgundy or dry white Bordeaux before red Bordeaux, red Burgundy, or sweet white Bordeaux
- Red Bordeaux before red Burgundy or sweet white Bordeaux
- Red Burgundy before sweet white Bordeaux.

An overriding rule is that a high-class wine should not be served before a less noble one. So, a lesser Bordeaux could perfectly well be served before an opulent, high-calibre Bordeaux. Finally, a young wine should precede an older one. However, one should not be a slave to these rules.

When it comes to Champagne, it would be a heresy to serve a *brut* at the end of the meal. Its place is at the very beginning, or even before. With dessert, sweet or medium sweet Champagne is more appropriate.

Dessert wines – Frontignan, Banyuls, sherry, Madeira or port – must come after all the others. Their high alcohol and sugar content completely ruin the tastebuds and make it impossible to appreciate the subtler qualities of the other wines. This brings us to the problem of an aperitif – it should be served long enough before the meal so as not to interfere with the tasting of the first wine that is served.

Good marriages

The following combinations of food and wine are suggested:

Oysters and shellfish

A dry white wine, such as a white Burgundy, a dry white Bordeaux (of which there are many that are excellent), an Alsace, a dry Touraine, a Muscadet, a Sancerre, a Pouilly-sur-Loire, a Pouilly-Fuissé (not to be confused with each other!), a Mâcon, a Chablis or a dry Jurançon.

Fish

- Grilled fish goes well with all the dry white or rosé wines (Provence, Tavel, etc).
- Fish served with a sauce prefers a wine which could even be used in the sauce itself – a rich, powerful dry white or a medium dry such as Vouvray or Anjou, or even a sweet wine in the case of a cream sauce.
- Smoked fish can only be served with a very dry, crisp, clean white wine that has a pronounced style such as a Sauvignon or an Alsace, rather than a delicate wine.
- Fish in red wine demands to be accompanied by a wine from the same *cru* as the wine in the sauce; Saint-Émilion or Pomerol, for example, would be good with lamprey.

Foie gras (goose liver pâté)

This is a thorny question, there being two irreconcilable schools of thought as to when *foie gras* should be served.

- For some, it makes a splendid beginning to a meal, and must be accompanied by a dazzling wine of a good lineage, such as Montrachet, Meursault, a good Chablis, Riesling or a well-chosen Gewurztraminer. A dry white Bordeaux would be equally welcome, although some 'experts' maintain that the only proper wine to serve with *foie gras* is a sweet Bordeaux: the majesty of the food, it is said, requires an exception to be made to the rules of good drinking. A wine that was not too sweet might prove to be an acceptable compromise.
- For those who believe in serving *foie gras* at the end of the meal the sweet whites of Bordeaux make it a magnificent experience.
- There are also those who feel that an elegant Bordeaux such as a Pomerol or a Saint Émilion is the ideal wine with *foie gras*.

Charcuterie

Young, aromatic wines such as Beaujolais, Côtes du Rhône, young red Loire wines, Côtes de Provence or even a light Bordeaux. Sauerkraut demands a white Alsace.

Truffles

Perfectly complemented by wines with a good bouquet, such as an older Bordeaux or Châteauneuf-du-Pape.

Dishes made with cream

These go well with sweet wines, such as a Bordeaux or an Anjou. *Vols-au-vent* and savoury pastries at the beginning of a meal may be accompanied by a medium dry white such as Vouvray, a Montlouis or even a Rosé d'Anjou, but that poses a problem for the rest of the meal. It would be better, especially if what follows will be rich, to turn to a distinctive white such as a Sauvignon or an Alsace.

French regional dishes

These usually have a distinctive character and are best accompanied by young aromatic wines from the area. Some examples are: Beaujolais with *saucisson chaud* (hot sausage), white Loire wines with buttered quenelles (fish balls),

Corbières or a Languedoc wine with *cassoulet*, medium dry Touraine wines with tripe. The exception is Normandy where the accepted accompaniment to any meal is cider.

Game

Game should always be accompanied by red wine, and the choice will depend on the delicacy or strength of the flavour of the meat. Game birds prefer a distinguished Burgundy such as a Beaune, a Santenay, a Volnay or a Côtes du Rhône that is not too heavy.

Larger game (such as venison) are well matched by the fuller bodied wines such as Pommard, Gevrey-Chambertin, Vosne-Romanée, Chambolle-Musigny and Châteauneuf-du-Pape.

Eggs

Egg dishes (soufflés, quiches, and so on) are good with all dry white wines.

Grills and roasts

- The delicate flavour of lamb likes a similarly light wine such as certain elegant red Graves or a good quality Volnay, Beaune or Savigny.
- White meat such as veal or poultry needs a wine which has a little more body but which is fairly light and refined. All the good wines of the Midi, Côtes du Rhône, the more modest Burgundies or the finest Bordeaux would all be suitable. The choice is wide here even if wines that are too aggressive are avoided.
- Red meats such as beef or mutton like to be supported by fuller bodied, more powerful wines such as Chinon, a good St-Nicolas-de-Bourgueil, the various types of Beaujolais (Morgon, Fleurie, Juliénas, Moulin à Vent) or the better Côtes du Rhône (Châteauneuf, Tavel, Hermitage); or choose from the long list of Bordeaux estates, or the Burgundies from the best villages of the slopes. The idea is to try to match the quality of the wine with that of the food.

Cheese

The choice of wine to accompany cheese is restricted by the fact that it comes at the end of the meal. It is often thought that any good red wine will do. But it is more subtle than that.

- Mild cheeses such as Tome de Savoie or Port Salut marry well with dry wines but also with young aromatic reds – Corbières, or the Beaujolais *crus*.
- Soft creamy cheeses of the Reblochon type go well with the fuller bodied whites such as a white Burgundy, dry white Bordeaux or Arbois, and also with the lighter Burgundies and Bordeaux.
- Soft strong cheeses such as Brie or Camembert are easier to please. All the dry whites or reds that have developed a bouquet are suitable (dry white Burgundy or Bordeaux, Arbois, or equally any red which has had a certain amount of time in the bottle).
- Hard cheeses, such as Gruyère or Comté prefer red wines with a fruity aroma or clean, crisp whites (Arbois or a good dry white Bordeaux).
- Blue cheeses such as Roquefort live happily with sweet white wines and full blooded reds. A Rosé d'Anjou would not be too outrageous.

- *Chèvre*, or goat's cheese, likes wines with a clean nose such as Sauvignon, Sancerre, Pouilly Fumé, a high class Beaujolais, Côtes du Rhône, Côtes de Provence or Côteaux de Languedoc.
- Strong cheeses must be accompanied by wines with a pronounced character and with plenty of body, such as Gewurztraminer with Munster, good quality sweet Bordeaux with Livarot, otherwise Epoisse, Maroilles or even Clos Vougeot, Chambertin, Châteauneuf-du-Pape or Madiran.

Desserts

Desserts are usually sweet and are only comfortable with dessert wines such as a good quality Anjou, Sauternes, Sainte-Croix-du-Mont, Monbazillac. This is also the moment to produce the Banyuls, Frontignans, ports and sweet sherries (keep the dry ones for the aperitif).

Bad marriages

- Only water should be served with a salad, or *vinaigrette hors-d'oeuvre.*
- Chocolate also does not go happily with wine, and cream is not much better.
- Red wine cringes at anything sweet or at cream sauces; neither should it be served with fish or shellfish, except when they are served with a special sauce.
- The true wine lover plans his menu according to the contents of his cellar rather than choosing the wines to suit the food.

It has been said that a meal should be like a symphony: the food is the melody and the wines provide the harmony. Creating a symphony may seem like hard work at first, but you will soon develop the instinct. And after all, wine is there to be enjoyed so choosing the one that you like may well be the best formula for success.

3
SERVING
WINE

The presentation of a drink as fine and subtle as wine, requires no props. In the past ornate tankards, chalices and goblets were highly regarded. In the Middle Ages an elaborate carafe would be much admired by guests at table, and there were extravagant arrangements such as that found at a banquet given in 1453 by the Duke of Burgundy: at each end of the table stood a statue of a lady whose breasts gave forth wine and a little boy who was peeing pink water. Like Dionysus, wine should be seen naked, without make-up or fancy dress. Clothes do not make the man, and the same is true of wine.

SERVING A SEQUENCE OF WINES

How many different wines should be served at one sitting? As few as possible.

One wine is not usually enough to meet the requirements of a menu. However, Champagne may well be used to accompany the whole meal providing you make sure you serve a medium dry or sweet with the dessert.

Two is usually the number to keep to. Three are sometimes necessary, but never more than that.

It is preferable to choose wines from the same vineyard; for example: a fine Médoc or Graves, followed by a powerful Saint-Émilion, and finally a Sauternes, or: a Meursault, followed by a Volnay, then a Pommard. But it is also possible to vary them: a Chassagne-Montrachet, a Médoc and finally an Anjou.

Two red wines from different origins always run the risk of detracting from one another.

THE GLASS

Wine must be drunk from a glass. Only glass allows one to get to the heart of the wine, to appreciate its clarity, its colour, and the various nuances of its texture. Of course, glass has only been available since the second half of the eighteenth century, and there are still many professional tasters who stick to the traditional 'taste-vin', but this is probably more for practical reasons than out of any technical advantages that this silver cup may have. It must be said in its favour, that metal does show up the colour tones well by the light that plays on the sides of the cup.

The wine glass must show off the wine to its best advantage without drawing attention to itself. The glass must therefore be fairly thin, colourless and transparent; it must have an elegant shape with a long enough stem for the fingers to be kept far away from the nose. The tulip shape is the best, with its slight narrowing towards the top which directs the fragrance towards the taster's nostrils. It is important for the glass to be large enough to swirl the wine around, to encourage the bouquet to be released. Ornamentation is unnecessary.

How many glasses should be put on the table? As many as there are wines, plus one for water.

It does not matter whether the glasses are of the same or different sizes. The fashion for keeping the smallest for a Bordeaux has no reason behind it.

A precaution worth taking is to smell the glasses carefully before using them. Some detergents and even chlorinated tap water, can leave behind odours which completely spoil the wine.

THE TEMPERATURE

This is the cause of much uncertainty and many a catastrophe. Above all, one must avoid extremes. Full bodied red wines should be served at room temperature, that is about 18–20 °C. It is a question of *chambrage*, that is bringing the wine gradually up to room temperature from the coolness of the cellar where it has been stored, and not a last-minute drastic heating up which would completely destroy the subtleties of the bouquet.

Lighter red wines can go down to 15 °C, and so can rosés.

On the other hand, whites should be drunk chilled, especially the dry ones. It is, however, important to remember that too much cold kills the nose and it is a sin to chill a wine by putting it into an ice bucket for too long. This piece of equipment should only be used in an emergency, and then only for whites; it is never needed for a bottle which has come out of a cool cellar. Wine gains nothing from being chilled to under 10 °C.

OPENING THE BOTTLE

This most delicate operation must be conducted with a great deal of care, without unduly disturbing the bottle or making the wine cloudy from the sediment that may have accumulated in the bottom. The use of a wine basket is recommended since it allows for the bottle that is to be opened to lie in an almost horizontal position.

The choice of corkscrew is important – it must not crush the cork, or damage it at all. Nothing is more disagreeable than for wine to be presented in a glass with bits of cork floating on its surface. The corkscrew should therefore be rigorously tested, but satisfactory models are rare. The corkscrew should go right through the cork, otherwise there is a risk of the cork breaking.

Wine is best presented very simply
(Photographs by Pierre Givet)

You should take care to smell the lower side of the cork to make sure that the wine does not have the catastrophic corked flavour. The cork's suppleness and quality should be inspected. It is quite right to be suspicious of the standard of a bottle stopped with a short cork, since all the *grands crus* have long ones.

One piece of advice: be careful with bottles of Champagne whose cork has broken, since a corkscrew could make the neck of the bottle explode and cause serious injuries. In no event should you use (gas) pressure corkscrews – you could have a bomb on your hands. A napkin placed like a scarf around the neck of the bottle is a sensible precaution.

When should the wine be opened? For an aromatic wine not long before serving, but for a bouquet wine never just before pouring it into glasses. And so we come to the controversial question of decanting wine.

DECANTING WINE

This is the process of transferring wine from the bottle into a carafe to serve it. Some claim that decanting is a mere affectation. Others claim that, far from being simply a ceremony, it is a necessity.

Only red wines with a bouquet should be decanted. Aromatic wines may be decanted in order to remove any sediment, but the procedure does not improve them in any way except to make them look more appealing. For bouquet wines it is a completely different matter: experience has shown that the precious bouquet which has been slowly developing in the bottle, and has been protected from the oxygen in the atmosphere, is greatly enhanced when the wine comes into contact with the air, but that this flame only lasts for a short while. It goes out quickly, and after it has been extinguished what is left is a flat, sour and flavourless liquid. It is important then to seize the exact moment to take advantage of this phenomenon which is still misunderstood by many wine lovers. The difficulty lies in pinpointing that moment, which occurs somewhere between fifteen minutes and two hours after decanting. As a rule of thumb, one could assume at least half an hour for a Burgundy and an hour for a Bordeaux.

The oldest wines have the most fragile bouquets and it is best to open them an hour before the meal and to decant them shortly before they appear on the table. White wines should also be opened an hour before serving, although they are less sensitive to contact with the air, being protected by the slight haze of sulphur that they usually have.

A wine that has been decanted must be drunk immediately, before it fades.

The procedure

- Stand the bottle upright for two days so that any sediment sinks to the bottom. Any deposit in the shoulder is known as *la mouche*.
- Rinse the carafe first in hot water and then with a small amount of suitable wine that is from the same region as the bottle to be decanted. Empty the carafe.
- Place it on the table with a candle burning behind it.
- If possible use a glass funnel – never a metal one – and very slowly pour the wine out, preferably letting it run down the side of the funnel.

- Continue to pour in one very slow gentle motion so as not to disturb the sediment. At all costs avoid the wine 'glugging' out of the bottle: it should flow smoothly from the bottle to the carafe.
- Tilt the bottle, all the time watching the liquid in the light of the flame.
- As soon as the first pieces of sediment appear in the neck, quickly turn the bottle upright. If the operation has been performed well, only a small amount of liquid will be left.

TASTING WINE

Serious wine tasting can only take place in a quiet, dignified atmosphere. It requires a certain amount of mental preparation. The din of a café, the frivolity of a club or the chatter of a banquet are not conducive to wine tasting. 'I can't hear myself drink', some comedian once said. And the room should be free of smokers and people wearing too much scent. On the other hand, wine tasting does not require the severity of a courtroom. All it asks for is a cheerful, inquisitive and anticipatory atmosphere.

The art of wine tasting involves so much subjectivity that descriptions are bound to be imprecise. Nevertheless, some reasonably objective characteristics can be found.

Firstly, the colour is easy to define and gives useful information about the age of the wine and how well it has been kept. The youngest red wines have purplish-blue reflections which develop into orange tones as they age.

Clarity is a sign of good health, but a slight cloudiness is not disastrous.

Although a sediment may look unpleasant, it does not usually affect the quality of a wine that has aged a little.

Next there is the nose, and here it is important to differentiate between the aroma and the bouquet, the former being sought after in young wines, the latter being absolutely necessary in older ones. The intensity of one or the other is not the only criterion of quality.

Then there is the actual taste of the wine which is more complex and therefore much more difficult to define. Acidity and sweetness each have measurable standards, such as naturally occurring acids and sugar. Two essential qualities are difficult to express; the body of a wine and the finesse of a wine. A full bodied wine is one that has some substance to it, creating an impression of richness and fullness in its composition. It is described as being rounded, robust, generous or even heady. The opposite of a full bodied wine is a light wine. This lightness can be an attractive, sought-after quality, but too much and you have a thin and empty wine.

The finesse of a wine is its charm, its distinction and its delicacy. It could be the dominant characteristic of a wine.

One must also consider the smoothness which sets a harsh wine apart from a soft wine; whether the wine is full flavoured or thin; and one should also note the finish of the wine, that is how long the taste remains in the mouth. One wine may fade quickly while another has a flourish or, as they say in France, *fait la queue de paon* (has a peacock's tail).

4

TALKING ABOUT
WINE

THE POETRY OF WINE

Through the ages wine has been talked about at great length. It has been the subject of poetry, prose and music. Whole anthologies have been devoted to the subject, from Homer to Baudelaire to Collette. Wine played a part in the great civilisations of Egypt, Greece and Rome, and the Church made a significant contribution to the creation of France's wines by sanctifying wine, the 'fruit of the earth and of man's labour'. Some Eastern religious groups, such as the Sufis, have also made wine a part of the mystical experience, the union with the divine. Aristophanes called wine 'the milk of Aphrodite', and the association of wine with the celebration of love has continued throughout history.

THE VOCABULARY OF WINE

Imagine the despair of a wine enthusiast who having chosen, nurtured and served a wine of very high calibre, hears the words, 'Not a bad bit of plonk!' On the other hand, it can be a delight, as André Maurois once wrote, 'to hear knowledgeable wine tasters talking with an almost religious fervour about a good bottle of wine'. Wine inspires some surprising descriptions: this one's got some meat, this one has a good panorama, this one puts sweaters on your teeth (heavy tannin). Wine tasting is a delicate business; it demands patience, taste and judgement. A taster of quality is an artist – one who has a heightened sense of the subtleties of the wine and is able to communicate his feelings to others.

Listed opposite are some of the adjectives used to describe wine. Observations are usually made in the order indicated here.

	Quality	Fault
Clarity:		
	clear	cloudy
	bright	dull
	pure	tainted
	transparent	opaque
Colour:		
	good colour	bad colour
	sumptuous	anaemic
	rich, ruby	washed out
Aroma:		
	a good nose	a closed-in nose
	good fruit	drying up
	delightful	boring
	attractive	thin
Bouquet:		
	has bouquet	is neutral
	sappy	underdeveloped
	striking	discreet
	forward	timid
	enchanting	dumb
	pungent	modest
General balance:		
	well-balanced	unbalanced
	well-resolved	unresolved
	rich	poor
	consistent	lacking shape
	full	thin
	distinctive	vulgar
	likeable	dull
	attractive	dreary
	delightful	undefined
	verve	flat
	striking	innocuous, uninspiring
	harmonious	uneven
	complete	austere
Cleanness or Crispness:		
	sound	burnt
	honest, clean	dirty
	crisp	subdued
	fresh	cooked, stewed, jammy
	correct	sour

This would be the place to reveal any possible bad flavours such as a corked wine, or a mousy flavour, or any unintentional flavours such as the foxiness of a hybrid, and so on.

Quality	Fault

Finesse:

Quality	Fault
refined	common
delicate	rough
elegant	tough
well bred, noble, distinguished	ordinary
vigorous	heavy
a lord	a ruffian
easy-going	stodgy

Body (or Fullness):

Quality	Fault
sturdy	(too) soft
well rounded, meaty	thin
solid	hollow
strong, powerful	weak
good weight, full bodied	(too) light
generous	sting
heady	feeble
opulent	flat

Style:

Quality	Fault
forward	timid
distinctive	uninspiring
expansive	shy
singular, original	without charm
stylish	insignificant
classy	unassuming
racy, inviting	austere
seductive	insipid
frivolous	serious
luscious	sad
uncompromising, straightforward	ordinary
gutsy	dreary
honest, simple, uncomplicated	overblown
gentle	aggressive

The flavour of the various soils may also be noted, such as the gun-flint of a Sauvignon, or the yellow flavour of an Arbois, the blackcurrant taste of a red Burgundy, a flavour of wood, resin, honey, spice, and so on.

	Quality	Fault
Acidity:		
	smooth	acidic, rough
	soft	hard, harsh, tart
	lively	sour, green
	nervy (as of horses)	soft, attenuated
	grassy	(too) sharp
Harshness (linked to the tannin content):		
	round	astringent
	gentle	hard
	velvet	biting
	creamy	tough
	silky	bitter
	thick	aggressive
	supple, smooth	harsh
Age:		
	young	old
	ripe	tired
	mature	(too) green, unripe
	green (white wine)	brown
	ruby, purple (red wine)	tawny

'Onion-skinned' (*pelure d'oignon*) is used to describe a well aged rosé wine that has a clear colour with orange tones.

Primeur or *nouveau* indicates a wine that is ready to drink immediately after the harvest.

The Finish:		
	long finish	short, stingy finish
	flourish	fades quickly

Long and complicated though this list may seem, it is not, of course, definitive. People will continue to find new imagery.

Before passing judgement, it is important to remember that:

- A high alcohol content accentuates sweetness.
- The flavours of sugar and acid cancel each other out.
- Sugar conceals a bitter flavour.

It has been said that the sweet flavour should balance out the flavours of acidity and bitterness.

Finally, it should be said that any judgement dictated by fashion or snobbishness is worthless. The best advice may be actually to say what you think.

5
STORING
WINE

SETTING UP A CELLAR

Bottles should always be stored horizontally.

A good cellar should be dark, since light is detrimental to the mysterious transformations of natural elements that give birth to the bouquet.

The temperature should be cool and, above all, stable; take, for instance, the famous Champagne *crayères*, underground cellars hidden under chalk masses that remain at around 12 °C throughout the year. Fluctuation between hot and cold upsets the wine's development.

Any movement is damaging: complete stillness is required for the liquid to clear and a sediment to form. This is why a compacted earth floor is preferable to a cement one which transmits every single tremor. A nearby road, railway line, or powerful motor can be disastrous. Any draughts which could cause the liquid inside the bottle to move slightly are to be avoided.

Damp conditions have a damaging effect on the works.

The cork fly is a formidable enemy. This little moth lays its eggs in the cork and the larvae then tunnel through it, sometimes reaching through to the wine which then begins to seep out. There are sprays which provide effective protection against this risk. In the popular image of a good cellar, the bottles are covered in spider's webs and coated with dust; a great bottle of wine is, of course, no less noble if it appears on the table clean. Finally, don't forget to keep your cellar securely locked.

CHOOSING WINE

Wine is not something that should be bought hastily, carelessly or blindly. It is important to find suppliers whom you can trust. If you do not take the trouble to do this, you may have the unhappy experience of inviting your guests to share with you a notable bottle of wine, and only then discover that the person who supplied it was a blundering incompetent or a swindler.

The trade name, although often decried, is a good guarantee in many cases: in Champagne, for instance. The only people who deserve your trust, be they retailers or producers, are those who have a reputation to keep up; those who are able to handle a criticism as well as a compliment, who take great care in serving you well, and serving the wine well, to whom you can go for information and advice, and who care about their customers.

Beware of aggressive or inaccurate advertising, and also of getting carried away at a wine fair and making purchases you may well regret the morning after.

Don't buy wine only a day or two before you mean to serve it. It is absolutely essential to let the wine rest for several days before serving it.

Bulk buying of wine in barrels or other containers is only satisfactory in the case of an aromatic wine bought for immediate consumption, or of a wine which is to be bottled immediately and stored. On no account should a large container be used to keep wine for several days at the family table. In less than twenty-four hours, a sour taste will appear, spoiling the remaining wine which will just deteriorate until it turns to vinegar.

Bottling wine at home

Bottling wine at home is a difficult process, and success cannot be guaranteed. If, however, you do wish to try your hand at bottling a small barrel of a *cru* that has captured your imagination, do take the following elementary precautions to avoid some of the hazards.

The cork
Always choose top quality corks. They can be fairly short if the wine is to be drunk soon but should be long if the wine is to be kept for several years.

Before use, the corks should be soaked in very hot water and left submerged for at least 24 hours. The cork should still be damp when used, but great care must be taken that, as it is put into the bottle, no water is squeezed into the wine.

The bottles
They should be of the conventional type – about 300 are needed for a 225 litre barrel. They should be washed in hot water, brushed, rinsed and left to drain before use. No detergent of any kind should be used.

The barrel
It should be completely full when delivered and show no signs of leaking; it should be properly spiked on top and bunged at the front. Once emptied, it is a good idea to rinse out the barrel, otherwise mould will start to grow, rendering it useless. A lit sulphured wick may then be inserted through the bung hole to ensure complete sterility.

The wine
First of all, it should rest for a few days somewhere where the temperature is right.

A laboratory analysis is highly recommended and the advice of a qualified wine expert is essential if disasters are to be avoided. You should obtain a 'bill of health' for your wine and, if necessary, a prescription for its treatment.

Some kind of fining will usually be necessary to remove any impurities. The simplest is to use egg whites for red wine (six egg whites per 225 litre barrel) and skimmed milk for white wine (half a litre per barrel). If powdered casein is available (15 g per 1000 litres) this is preferable for both red and white wines.

To carry out the operation, the barrel is placed in a perfectly horizontal position on a prop which is about 50 cm high. Using a special piece of equipment, the barrel is uncorked and one or two litres of wine are run off; then if egg whites have been used, the wine now receives an additional fining of two or three pinches of salt. It should then be stirred vigorously with a special curved whisk and allowed to rest for about three weeks. Ideally, the wine should then be racked off into another sterilised barrel, taking great care not to stir up the lees. It can be siphoned off quite simply by attaching a piece of rubber tubing to a wooden stick and placing this in such a way as to leave about 10–15 cm between the end of the tubing and the bottom of the barrel. If it is not possible to transfer the wine to another barrel, it can be put straight into bottles. A wooden tap is driven into the bung hole with a sharp tap from a wooden mallet, taking care not to disturb the barrel. A small bowl placed underneath the tap will catch any wine that overflows from the bottles. The wine may now be drawn off, but only if it looks perfectly clear. If it does not, you will have to wait for a few days to allow the lees to sink down to the bottom. It can happen, unfortunately, that the wine remains cloudy, and in this case you will have to seek advice from an expert.

The bottling process

Once clear, the wine is drawn off into bottles. The liquid should come high enough up the neck of the bottle to leave a space of two to three centimetres between the wine and the cork. The operation should be carried out without interruption as prolonged exposure to the air is extremely detrimental.

Draw the wine off for as long as it runs clear and cork each bottle immediately with a corking device that lets air escape as the cork is pushed in. As soon as the flow slows down, very carefully and with the help of an assistant raise the rear of the barrel until the wine, which will now be cloudy, appears in the tap. Replace the barrel and collect the lees which can be strained through a cloth and used in cooking.

All these procedures must be carried out with the utmost care; failures are usually due to negligence or to error, such as allowing metal instruments to come into contact with the wine.

Finally, any wine that is bottled at home needs to be laid down for long enough to eliminate the unpleasant taste which it acquires during that process because of the air that becomes dissolved in it. This is a bottle sickness that is familiar to specialists and can take six months to a year to disappear.

There is no point in denying the fact that amateur wine bottling is risky, so complex is the science of wine and so great its subtlety. Many professionals too have had their failures, and the best advice is to leave bottling to the experts.

MANAGING YOUR CELLAR

You must keep a constant eye on your cellar; wine often develops very quickly. This is true of most aromatic wines – many of the good Languedoc or

Provençal wines lose their charm after the first heat of summer. It is also advisable to drink *vins primeurs* (new wines) before the end of the winter so as to make the most of all their attractive qualities and their delicate freshness. Even wines with a bouquet are not immortal; they blossom slowly, reach their peak and then begin a decline which can be quite rapid.

Champagne can only be kept for a few years, white Burgundies a little longer. The great white sweet Bordeaux and sweet Anjous may be kept for several decades. Among red wines the Bordeaux are the ones most suited to old age, but only a few real champions are able to stay in good shape into their fifties. Burgundies should be watched more closely since they do not easily adapt to old age.

A true wine lover takes great care not to allow the best pieces of his collection to reach the point of decrepitude. It has been said that wine should be mature, but not senile.

6

WHAT IS
WINE?

THE VINE

A vine is simply a creeper that has the fortunate capacity of producing pleasant fruits. There are various genera, sub-genera, species and varieties of the *Ampelidaceae* family, but only the *vitis* is of interest here; the rest of these green creepers are simply ornamental. There are various types of *vitis* which play an important role in viticulture, including *vitis vinifera, vitis riparia, vitis rupestris* and *vitis labrusca.*

The first of these, *vitis vinifera* (called *vigne française* in France), groups together all the varieties that are used in wine production in France. These are Pinot, Gamay, Cabernet Franc, Cabernet-Sauvignon, Chardonnay, Chenin, Muscadet, Riesling, Gewurztraminer, and so forth, each one being well adapted to a particular region by its affinity with the elements in the soil, its adaptation to the climate or its resistance to certain diseases. These *vinis vinifera* types are exclusively authorised to be used in vineyards that produce *appellation contrôlée* wines, *vins delimités de qualité supérieure*, or *vins de pays.*

Unfortunately, these vines suffer from one big disadvantage – they are not resistant to phylloxera, the small insect whose larvae stick to the roots, suck out the sap and kill the plant. The whole of France was invaded by this undesirable creature between 1878 and 1892. Some form of protection had to be found, and it was discovered that resistance to disease could be achieved by grafting French vines on to another type of *vitis*; this grafting stock could be practically any except the *vinifera.*

But grafting is a delicate and laborious process, and researchers turned their attention to the creation of hybrids by crossing *vitis vinifera* with a more resistant species. This is done by sprinkling the pollen from the flowers of one species on to the pistils of the other in order to obtain a hybrid seed or pip. Grafting became more or less obsolete, and these cross-pollenated hybrids experienced considerable success. Within a quarter of a century they had been planted in almost one-fifth of the vineyards of France, primarily in the northernmost regions.

Unfortunately, the quality of the wine suffered badly and the legislature had to intervene to put a stop to this invasion. Some hybrids were totally forbidden, others were tolerated and a few favoured ones were actually accepted, although these were the ones which had the least resistance to phylloxera. Today they have declined significantly in number and are only found in a few scattered vineyards and used in the production of *vin de consommation courante*. They will continue to decline in importance since, apart from a few authorised exceptions, it is now forbidden to plant them.

It is a sad fact about French vines that the prolific varieties are not those that produce the best wines, quantity and quality being incompatible – to the great sorrow of the winemaker. In Languedoc the gradual descent of the generous Aramon vine from the hills down to the fertile plains was one of the misfortunes of the Midi. Cultivation that is too intensive is also damaging.

It is interesting to note how the same plant cultivated in different areas can produce completely different results, as in the case of the Sauvignon in Bordeaux and in the Loire valley; of the jurassic Savagnin which becomes Traminer in Alsace; and of the Melon of Burgundy which becomes Muscadet in Nantais.

VITICULTURE

As with any type of cultivation, a good harvest requires hard work.

Firstly, the land usually has to be worked so as to aerate the soil, conserve its water reserves, and kill any harmful weeds. The vines are earthed up in winter and uncovered in summer so as to make more use of the seasonal rains. Labour-free cultivation with the help of just chemical weedkillers is, of course, increasing gradually.

Fertilisers are essential because in time the soil becomes drained of nutrients. Potassium helps to improve the quality of the soil; nitrogen and organic matter

Fermenting must
(Photograph by Pierre Mackiewicz – Institut Technique du Vin)

sustain the plant, and phosphates help them to do this. Fertiliser that is too rich can have unwanted effects: for instance, grapes may rot and the quality of the wine may be reduced. Irrigation encourages overproduction, and is strictly regulated.

Vines used to be planted very close together, but mechanisation of production has meant that wider spaces are now left between the stocks to allow tractors to pass through; at the same time each stock is required to bear more fruit to maintain the yield.

Pruning is critical in regulating production. Enough buds must be left to ensure a good harvest, but too many would yield too large a number of grapes to be compatible with good quality.

Vine props and iron wire hold up the plant, but this should not be an excuse to allow the vine to grow ridiculously tall. Pruning at leaf stage removes foliage that is superfluous or is hindering fruit growth by keeping the grapes in the shade.

Winemakers have to struggle against various diseases that can attack the vine. Many diseases are caused by deficiencies or excesses in the soil; for example, the amount of calcium in the soil in Cognac is very high and vines have to be sprayed so as to prevent the leaves turning yellow.

Climatic conditions can cause serious losses, and prevention or reduction of such losses is more difficult; netting is used against hail, heaters and smoke against frost. Nothing can be done to prevent rain from falling on the flower, destroying its fertility.

Animal parasites do not pose a great threat these days. Phylloxera has been wiped out by a process of grafting the vines on to certain stocks; cochylis, eudemis, and one or two other small moths still exist, but these are easily killed off by insecticides.

There are also various moulds; these are the biggest threat and have to be carefully watched out for. Mildew, black-rot and oidium are all capable of ruining an entire crop in just a few days. Fungicides offer fairly effective protection. However the rotting of the grape in poor weather which spoils the harvest remains a scourge that is difficult to control despite the lengthy measures taken against it. The winemaker has to keep a daily lookout for the first threads on the underside of the leaves, the first marks or blemishes on the bunches. A successful harvest depends on the winemaker's constant vigil.

Harvest is a day of festivity but also a day of anxiety. Are the grapes really just right? Has enough of the acid disappeared and is the sugar inside the berries concentrated enough? Is the fruit healthy enough or will it impart mouldy or rotten flavours, giving as one says euphemistically, *le gout de l'année*? Are the grape-pickers competent? Will they see their work through to the end? Will rain stop work and dilute the juice, and is the estimated alcohol content sufficient? Is the winery big enough? Such questions haunt the winemaker as he prepares to reap the fruits of a year's labour. A hailstorm at the last minute can be a tragedy. On the other hand, if all goes well, the winemaker's happiness is immense, and there is singing and laughter all day long.

In Bordeaux especially great care is taken in the harvesting of grapes for sweet white wine. The grapes that are selected must be sweet enough to leave behind large enough amounts of sugar after fermentation to give the sweetness and richness of a Sauternes, for example. The juice is left in the grape to become concentrated by the effect of a fungus *botrytis cinerea*, noble rot. The grapes have to be picked one by one, as the mould spreads. Each bunch has to be visited several – maybe seven or eight – times. The harvest requires time and skills that only a few great estates can still afford, and these traditional methods may not survive much longer. We may soon see the disappearance from the vineyards of all craftsmen, and a complete takeover by mechanised production.

HOW WINE IS MADE

Oenology is both the art and the science of wine. The vast amount of work taking place in laboratories and in specially equipped cellars is making winemaking more and more of a science. But there are still many aspects which have not been reduced to scientific fact and remain in the realm of art.

Once the grapes have been harvested the winemaking process continues according to whether the wine is to be white, red or rosé, dry or sweet, light or full bodied, and so on.

For a red wine, the grapes are crushed and stemmed and the must (the combination of juice, skins and pips) is put into fermentation vats. For a white wine, the grapes have first to go to a press to separate the clear juice from the skins. This operation has to be performed quickly and in such a way that the liquid that goes into the vats is not contaminated by the dyes in the skins. In Champagne, pressing is done in several stages. When all the juice from the first pressing (the *vin de cuvée*) has been extracted, the press is stopped and the pulp from around the edges of the press is partially broken up and mixed back into the liquid. A second pressing then follows, producing the *premiere taille*, the highest quality run-off. A second quality run-off is produced in the same way, but is generally not included in the blend or *cuvée*. Finally, a third vigorous pressing produces low quality wine which is contaminated by dye and is used separately, never for Champagne.

Presses currently in use are chiefly of the horizontal type which have automatic equipment for breaking up the pulp.

For both whites and reds, the next stage is fermentation. A small amount of sulphur dioxide is added to kill off any undesirable bacteria and wild yeasts, and to protect against the harmful effects of oxidation. Wine yeasts may be added. Fermentation must begin quickly. It is a complicated chemical process: put very simply, the yeast transforms the sugar in the grapes into alcohol and carbon dioxide.

Fermentation causes a rise in temperature which has to be controlled so that the activity of the yeast does not slow down or, worse still, stop altogether. This would happen at around 40 °C and the result would be a sickly-sweet wine, good only for vinegar.

The liquid has to be aerated during the fermentation, and this is done by pumping liquid from the bottom of the vat back over the layer of grape solids floating on the top – the *chapeau*, cap.

This first fermentation, called *tumultueuse* because of the noise made by escaping gas, only lasts a few days. The vat is then emptied and the wine will be finished off in barrels.

If red wine is being made, the pulp is taken from the vat and put through the press again to produce a 'pressed' wine, as opposed to the better 'free run' wine already obtained.

For a sweeter wine, the wine is transferred to barrels before all the sugar has been converted into alcohol and is then stabilised by a further addition of sulphur dioxide.

Increasingly, conveyor-belt equipment is being used, allowing for continuous production from beginning to end.

STORAGE IN VATS, CASKS AND BARRELS

The primary reason for storing wine at this stage in vats, casks or barrels is to complete the fermentation process which, in the case of dry wines, has to be total; only minute traces of sugar may be allowed to remain (one or two grams per litre). In this second stage of fermentation the harsh, bitter malic acid initially present in the wine is converted to the softer, more acceptable lactic acid. This malolactic fermentation is caused by the action of micro-organisms, and usually needs protection and a helping hand.

The new wine is left for a while, and then racked again to separate it from the lees that have settled at the bottom of the vat.

The process is still far from finished: the wine is unstable, it is evolving, and, like every living organism, it has its period of youth, maturity and senility, and eventually it dies. It has been said that, left to nature, wine would become vinegar, and bad vinegar at that! This must be avoided at all costs, and it is the winemaker's skill which allows the wine to realise its true potential. His objective at all times is to preserve the charms of the wine. He is not a manufacturer. The wine given to him by nature is well protected by its alcohol, its tannin and its acids. The winemaker's task is to bring out some of the many substances that wine naturally comprises; nearly 400 substances have been counted, and research may yet reveal many more. Some characteristics are eliminated, some are emphasised. In addition, the wine has to be protected against spoilage.

What methods does the winemaker use? Before or during fermentation, some harvests that are too weak may be enriched by the addition of either grape concentrate or sugar (chaptalisation). Similarly, the addition or removal of acid may be permitted to a limited extent. These procedures are only allowed in areas with unfavourable growing conditions, within well defined limits and conditions, and only during the winemaking process.

Other handling procedures that are permitted are: racking, ullage (the topping up of the barrels as the wine evaporates), blending, filtering and fining. Fining involves adding a gelatinous sticky substance that floats through the liquid, taking any impurities down to the lees.

Heat treatments – refrigeration pasteurisation, extreme heat or cold – are also used to try and protect or improve the product.

One or two natural substances are sometimes used: for instance, pure clay or bentonite can help clarify a wine; gum arabic or citric acid help maintain the

Pumping wine from the bottom of the vat back over the cap (Château Canon, Bordeaux)
(Photograph by J. P. Verney – Ministry of Agriculture archives)

brightness of white wines; metatartaric acid helps to prevent crystallisation (this is simply the wine's own natural tartaric acid which is heated to modify its properties); and vitamin C (or ascorbic acid) and sorbic acid, which guard against accidental refermentation.

Lastly, there are two treatments which have attracted great criticism. Sulphur dioxide: it must be said that this does not improve the smell, the aroma, or the bouquet. Nevertheless, wine is a perishable commodity and some kind of anhydrous sulphate acts as both antiseptic and antioxidant. It is a small evil and an ancient method; every Frenchman remembers the sulphured wick that his grandfather used to use. If used with caution, the taste eventually disappears.

Metals cause cloudiness, making the wine opaque, and they must be removed by blue fining. Of all the practices, this is the least offensive despite the horrific name of the product used: potassium ferrocyanide. It may only be done under the control of a qualified oenologist.

WINE DISEASES

These can be divided into three types. First, there are unwanted flavours which develop if the wine is not well kept, or from the grapes having been spoiled: mould, rot, flavour of lees, a yeast flavour, a paraffin flavour, a corked flavour, and so on. Second, there are the microbial diseases that Louis Pasteur discovered: the 'flower', the whitish growth on the surface of a wine that has been badly stored; the 'sting', or the development of wine into vinegar that produces a sharp flavour; and souring and bitterness, both of which are caused by the development of micro-organisms; there is also oiliness which makes the wine chewy and sticky. In this category one could also include accidental refermentation in wines that still have sugar or malic acid present. Modern winemaking techniques have reduced the number of microbial diseases, but their effects remain unaltered. The third type of 'disease' is the result of various natural components interacting with each other under the influence of cold or heat, or simply due to the passage of time. For example, deposits of tartaric crystals; or cloudiness due to metals (generally iron or copper), proteins, colourants or diastases.

Despite the serious nature of some of these problems, they are all controllable and no corrective treatment allowed by law is dangerous.

YOUR GOOD HEALTH!

'Wine is the healthiest and most hygienic of all drinks.' This was the opinion of Louis Pasteur, a man who contributed as much as anybody in history to the health of mankind, and it still holds true today. And we should not forget that it was wine that put Louis Pasteur on the road to his discoveries.

'Your good health!' we say, as we raise our glasses, and these words may be taken literally.

The incidence of cirrhosis is frequently blamed on wine drinking, but it is a fact that, in France, this disease is least prevalent in the big wine producing and consuming regions of the south and most common in non-wine growing regions.

Wine is really a most valuable food. It has a significant calorific value and numerous beneficial effects upon the organism; it is rich in vitamins, and has antiseptic and bactericidal properties. There are two antibiotics that are only found in wine: botryticine and a certain aglucone.

WINE AND THE LAW

'No drink may be produced, kept or transported for the purpose of sale, or distributed, auctioned or retailed under the name of wine unless it has been produced exclusively by the fermentation of fresh grapes or grape juice.' Thus states Article 1 of the *Code du Vin*. But the French legislature does not stop there. There is a whole set of legislation surrounding wine. Few consumable goods in France are so regulated, defined, supervised, monitored, sampled, analysed and judged. In addition to the national rules, which are always being modified, local legislatures apply their own rules and regulations. You can be sure that, as a result of all this, the consumer is extremely well protected.

It requires enormous ingenuity to perpetrate a wine fraud. There are so many organisations controlling the industry that fraud on a large scale is virtually impossible. Such fraud as does exist tends to concern alcoholic strength, misleading labels, or dubious origins. There is no question of selling wine that is being made from something that could damage public health.

So, as an old wine promotion slogan had it: 'Drink wine and live happily.'

PART II

BORDEAUX

'Bordeaux' is now used to describe all the wines from the department of Gironde with the exception of a few wooded parishes adjacent to the department of Landes. Formerly it referred to the wines from the town of Bordeaux itself, which were accorded preferential treatment; wines belonging to the city's *négociants* were sold first, and neighbouring areas were only allowed to offer their wine at certain times and could only sell them in Bordeaux after the priority wines had been sold.

GROWING CONDITIONS

The soil is varied; water-deposited alluvium along the rivers, clay and limestone on the slopes of the eastern bank of the Garonne, sand and gravel in Médoc. These last are typical of the great estates of high renown: huge expanses of round pebbles – quartz, often translucent – accumulated by the river over a long period of geological time and now resting on a bed of sand or clay.

The Aquitaine climate is maritime: damp, quite warm, subject to spring frosts but often having the benefit of splendid autumns.

Most of the vines planted here are Cabernet-Sauvignon, Cabernet franc, red Merlot, Carmenère, Malbec and Petit-Verdot for red wines, and Semillon, Sauvignon and Muscadelle for whites, although Mauzac, Colombard, Ugni and a few others may be added to table wines.

THE *CRUS*

Appellations d'origine contrôlées

These account for 70 per cent of the total production; about two-thirds are red and one-third white.

Bordeaux
This is the general *appellation* given to all wines produced within the defined area that have an alcoholic strength of 10° for reds and dry whites, 10.5° for

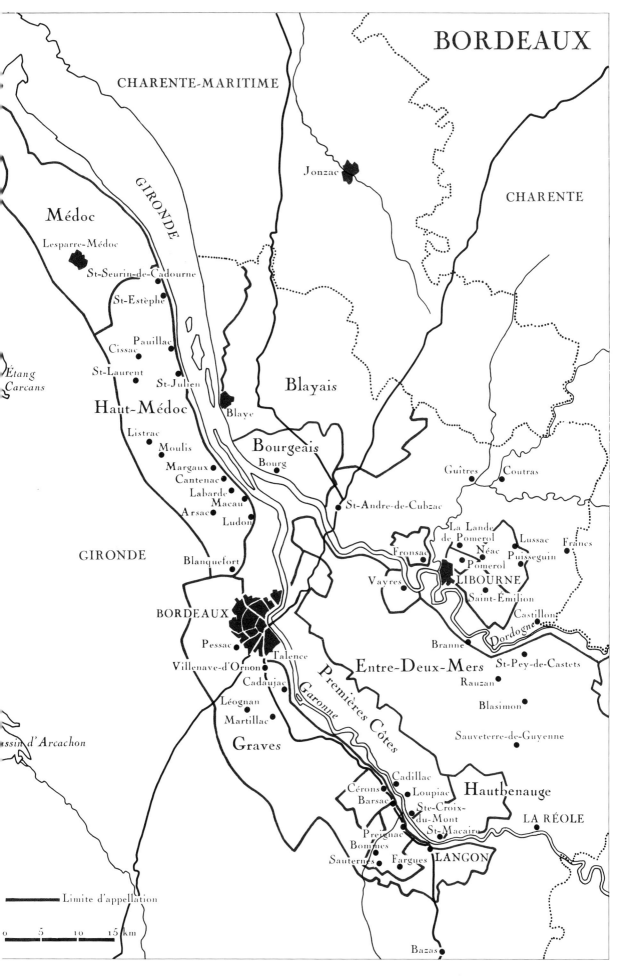

BORDEAUX

CHARENTE-MARITIME

CHARENTE

GIRONDE

Médoc

Jonzac

Lesparre-Médoc

St-Seurin-de-Cadourne

St-Estèphe

Cissac

Pauillac

Étang
Carcans

St-Laurent

St-Julien

Blayais

Haut-Médoc

Blaye

Listrac

Bourgeais

Moulis

Bourg

Margaux

Cantenac

Guîtres

Coutras

Labarde

Macau

St-André-de-Cubzac

Arsac

Ludon

La Lande
de Pomerol

Lussac

Francs

GIRONDE

Fronsac

Néac

Puisseguin

Pomerol

Blanquefort

Vayres

LIBOURNE

Saint-Émilion

Castillon

BORDEAUX

Dordogne

Pessac

Branne

St-Pey-de-Castets

Talence

Entre-Deux-Mers

Villenave-d'Ornon

Rauzan

Cadaujac

Premières Côtes

Blasimon

Léognan

Garonne

Martillac

Sauveterre-de-Guyenne

ssin d'Arcachon

Graves

Cadillac

Cérons

Loupiac

Hautbenauge

Barsac

Ste-Croix-
du-Mont

St-Macaire

LA RÉOLE

Preignac

Bommes

LANGON

Sauternes

Fargues

Bazas

Limite d'appellation

0   5   10   15 km

sweet whites (they actually reach 10°), and 11° for rosés. They are produced from authorised vines and within a limit of maximum yield per hectare which varies from year to year but averages 65 hectolitres.

The quality of the wines produced under this label is extremely variable because of the many different sources.

Bordeaux reds are characterised by a distinctive strength or power, caused by their high tannin content, which can sometimes go as far as harshness or toughness. Their alcoholic strength is only average, and adding sugar to the harvest is usually authorised (within the limits of necessary correction). The winemaker has to rely mostly on the sugar that the grape contains.

These are good sound wines that age well, are rarely affected by disease, and usually require a certain amount of ageing in the bottle. Despite the charm of one or two smaller *crus* they do not make good *primeurs* (new wines), but do acquire an excellent bouquet.

Faults to watch out for are the thinness of bad years, harshness brought about by being kept in the vat for too long, and the unpleasant taste, if pronounced, of a wine from alluvial soils.

The white wines may be dry or sweet. The sweet wines are more traditional although production is declining significantly at the moment. They are soft, fruity and improve by being kept in the bottle for a while to allow the sulphurous smell to disappear: this smell can be a problem but, happily, it usually turns into an exceptional bouquet.

Bordeaux supérieur is the *appellation* reserved for wines with an alcoholic strength of at least 10.5°. These are grown on the same land but with a smaller yield per hectare and from specially selected vines. In general they are good wines that should be left for a few months and which would make a very good foundation for anyone's cellar. Whites are not very common.

Château d'Yquem (Sauternes)
(Photograph by Pierre Mackiewicz – Institut Technique du Vin)

Production of *Bordeaux clairet* is small, and the wine is rarely exported. It has a light colour, somewhere between red and rosé, charm and elegance.

Bordeaux rosé is similarly not produced in large quantities. Lighter in colour and substance than the clairet, it is not unattractive if it comes from a good producer.

Bordeaux Sauvignon is a dry white aromatic wine that is delicate and refined; in a good year it is just as good as a Loire Sauvignon.

Bordeaux mousseux is made from white Bordeaux using the champagne method of secondary fermentation in the bottle. It has not yet achieved great renown, which is perhaps a shame.

Médoc

The official *appellation* area is confined to the peninsula bordered on the east by Gironde and Garonne, to the south by Blanquefort (some 10 kilometres to the north of the town of Bordeaux) and to the west by the ocean, with the exception of the communes next to the coastal lakes which are situated on young alluvial stable soils on top of an impermeable bedrock.

The wines found here are almost entirely red, Cabernet Franc and Cabernet-Sauvignon being the predominant grapes. These give the wine a great solidity, fullness, richness and excellent ageing potential.

Haut Médoc comprises the southern part of Médoc, from Saint-Seurin-de-Cadourne to Blanquefort. This is where the most prestigious *crus* are found: Margaux, known for its extreme finesse; Pauillac for its body and richness; Saint-Estèphe for its grapiness and its power; and Saint-Julien and Cantenac where these qualities always seem to be evenly distributed.

The following should also be mentioned: Ludon, Saint-Laurent, Labarde, Macau, Listrac and Moulis.

In a good year, a collection of truly extraordinary qualities can be found here – verve, elegance, harmony, class – all of which combine to make the great label of Médoc the most illustrious coat of arms in wine heraldry.

An official classification, dating from 1855, has ranked the greatest of the *crus*; since this time changes have taken place and amalgamations have been authorised, sometimes very large ones, leading to improvements as well as to deteriorations in quality.

PREMIERS GRANDS CRUS:

Château Lafite-Rothschild   Pauillac
Château Latour   Pauillac
Château Margaux   Margaux
Château Mouton-Rothschild   Pauillac

DEUXIÈMES GRANDS CRUS:

Château Rausan-Ségla   Margaux
Château Rausan-Gassies   Margaux
Château Léoville-Las-Cases   Saint-Julien
Château Léoville-Poyferré   Saint-Julien
Château Léoville-Barton   Saint-Julien

Château Durfort-Vivens   Margaux
Château Lascombes   Margaux
Château Gruaud-Larose   Saint-Julien
Château Brane-Cantenac   Cantenac
Château Pichon-Longueville   Pauillac
Château Pichon-Longueville
    (Comtesse de Lalande)   Pauillac
Château Ducru-Beaucaillou   Saint-Julien
Château Cos-d'Estournel   Saint-Estèphe
Château Montrose   Saint-Estèphe

TROISIÈMES GRANDS CRUS:

Château Kirwan   Cantenac
Château d'Issan   Cantenac
Château Lagrange   Saint-Julien
Château Langoa   Saint-Julien
Château Giscours   Labarde
Château Malescot-Saint-Exupéry   Margaux
Château Cantenac-Brown   Cantenac
Château Palmer   Cantenac
Château La Lagune   Ludon
Château Desmirail   Margaux
Château Calon-Ségur   Saint-Estèphe
Château Ferrière   Margaux
Château Marquis-d'Alesme-Becker   Margaux
Château Boyd-Cantenac   Margaux

QUATRIÈMES GRANDS CRUS:

Château Saint-Pierre-Sevaistre   Saint-Julien
Château Branaire-Ducru   Saint-Julien
Château Talbot   Saint-Julien
Château Duhart-Milon   Pauillac
Château Pouget   Cantenac
Château La Tour-Carnet   Saint-Laurent
Château Lafon-Rochet   Saint-Estèphe
Château Beychevelle   Saint-Julien
Château Le Prieuré-Lichine   Cantenac
Château Marquis-de-Termes   Margaux

CINQUIÈMES GRANDS CRUS:

Château Pontet-Canet   Pauillac
Château Batailley   Pauillac
Château Haut-Batailley   Pauillac
Château Grand-Puy-Lacoste   Pauillac
Château Grand-Puy-Ducasse   Pauillac
Château Lynch-Bagues   Pauillac

Château Lynch-Moussas   Pauillac
Château Dauzac   Labarde
Château Moutone-Baron-Philipe   Pauillac
Château Le Tertre   Arsac
Château Haut-Bages-Liberal   Pauillac
Château Pédesclaux   Pauillac
Château Belgrave   Saint-Laurent
Château Camensac   Saint-Laurent
Château Cos-Labory   Saint-Estèphe
Château Clerc-Milon-Mondon   Pauillac
Château Croizet-Bages   Pauillac
Château Cantemerle   Macau

Apart from this large, revered body of *grands crus*, Médoc includes some respectable dignitaries. These are known as *crus grands bourgeois exceptionelles*:

Château Agassac   Ludon
Château Andron-Blanquet   Saint-Estèphe
Château Beausite   Saint-Estèphe
Château Capbern   Saint-Estèphe
Château Caronne-Sainte-Gemme   Saint-Laurent
Château Chasse-Spleen   Moulis
Château Cissac   Cissac
Château Le Crock   Saint-Estèphe
Château Dutruch-Grands-Poujeaux   Moulis
Château Fourcas-Dupré   Listrac
Château Fourcas-Hosten   Listrac
Château Du Glana   Saint-Julien
Château Haut-Marbuzet   Saint-Estèphe
Château Marbuzet   Saint-Estèphe
Château Meyney   Saint-Estèphe
Château Phélan-Ségur   Saint-Estèphe
Château Poujeaux   Moulis

To this list of *crus* judged 'exceptional' by their syndicate in 1978 should be added:

Château D'Angludet   Cantenac
Château Gloria   Saint-Julien
Château Bel-Air-Marquis-d'Aligre   Soussans
Château Fonreaud   Listrac
Château Bellegrave   Listrac
Château Colombier-Monpelou   Pauillac
Château La Couronne   Pauillac
Château Fonbadet   Pauillac
Château de Labegorce   Margaux
Château de Labegorce Zédé   Margaux
Château Lanessan   Cussac

Château Les-Ormes-de-Pez   Saint-Estèphe
Château de Pez   Saint-Estèphe
Château Phélan-Ségur   Saint-Estèphe
Château Siran   Margaux
Château Tronquoy-Lalande   Saint-Estèphe
Château Villegeorge   Avensan

and it is cruel to have to stop there.

Within Haut Médoc, some of the better known communes are able to classify their wine under a more specific *appellation contrôlée*, providing it conforms to certain standards, including having an alcoholic strength of at least 10.5°:

Pauillac
Margaux
Saint-Julien
Saint-Estèphe
Moulis: produces solid, meaty wines
Listrac: produces well rounded and elegant wines

Graves

This *appellation* applies to the vineyard that in the north begins right in the suburbs of Bordeaux and stretches southwards as far as Langon, covering about 40 communes. Both red and white wines are found. The reds are noteworthy wines that can stand comparison with the great Médocs, having perhaps a little less roundness but possessing an elegance and grace that would prompt one to describe them as feminine. Their silkiness and velvety quality are beyond compare.

Since 1959, the classification is as follows:

Château Haut-Brion   Pessac
(This extremely prestigious *cru* had been classed as the *premier cru* of Gironde since 1855, and was moreover the only Graves mentioned.)

Château Haut-Bailly   Léognan
Château La Mission-Haut-Brion   Talence
Château Latour-Haut-Brion   Talence
Château Carbonnieux   Léognan
Domaine de Chevalier   Léognan
Château Malartic-Lagravière   Léognan
Château Olivier   Léognan
Château La Tour-Martillac   Martillac
Château-Smith-Haut-Lafitte   Martillac
Château Bouscaut   Cadaujac
Château Pape-Clément   Pessac
Château Fieuzal   Léognan

There are no *crus bourgeois* in Graves, but the following deserve a mention:

Château Larrivet-Haut-Brion   Léognan
Château Le Désert   Léognan

Château Haut-Gardère   Léognan
Château La Louvière   Léognan
Château Baret   Villenave-d'Ornon
Château Pontac-Montplaisir   Villenave-d'Ornon
Château L'Hermitage   Martillac
Château Lognac   Castres

Unfortunately Graves dry whites go unnoticed by many wine lovers. They are, however, remarkable wines with a good bouquet, very subtle and with a certain attractiveness that makes them an excellent accompaniment to seafood.

Apart from the incomparable but unobtainable white Haut-Brion, the official classification names the following:

Château Carbonnieux   Léognan
Château Bouscaut   Cadaujac
Domaine de Chevalier   Léognan
Château Olivier   Léognan
Château Laville-Haut-Brion   Pessac and Talence
Château Malartic-Lagravière   Léognan
Château Couhins   Villenave-d'Ornon
Château La Tour-Martillac   Martillac

to which may be added the more modest *crus*:

Château La Blancherie   La Brède
Château Ferrande   Castres
Château Malleprat   Martillac
Château Raoul   Portets

The most prestigious sweet white wines of this region simply appear under their own particular name, such as Sauternes or Barsac. But to the north, in the

Pourriture Noble (Sauternes)
(Photograph by Pierre Mackiewicz –
Institut Technique du Vin)

region of the so-called Petits Graves, there are some pleasant and rich wines, the best known being *Cérons*.

The *appellation Graves supérieurs* is restricted to white wines that meet certain standards, one of which is to have a total alcohol content of 12°; they are sweeter than plain Graves.

Sauternes and Barsac

The area of these greatly renowned *appellations* is actually within Graves close to the River Garonne. Semillon and Sauvignon, along with a few rare Muscadelle stocks produce these very good sweet wines.

The vines are pruned right back so that their yield is greatly reduced, to around 25 hectolitres per hectare. For the best *crus* the grapes are not gathered until they have been affected by noble rot, and are gathered in successive pickings so as to choose the individual grapes that have rotted to a satisfactory degree, reducing their volume by approximately two-thirds.

Smooth sweetness is not the only quality that these wines possess; their great finesse, their bouquet, their vigour, their creaminess, all combine to make some admirable wines.

A dislike of sweet wines among certain wine drinkers is very regrettable, when one considers the work and the sacrifices that a winemaker has to endure in order to obtain this very high quality.

Barsac wines are more heady, Sauternes more vigorous and elegant.

The official classification was completed in 1855.

PREMIER GRAND CRU:

Château d'Yquem   Sauternes

PREMIERS CRUS:

Château La Tour-Blanche   Bommes
Château Lafaurie-Peyraguey   Bommes
Clos Haut Peyraguey   Bommes
Château Rayne-Vigneau   Bommes
Château Rabaud-Promis   Bommes
Château Suduiraut   Preignac
Château Coutet   Barsac
Château Climens   Barsac
Château Guiraud   Sauternes
Château Rieussec   Fargues
Château Sigalas-Rabaud   Bommes

DEUXIÈMES CRUS:

Château Doisy-Daëne   Barsac
Château Doisy-Dubroca   Barsac
Château Doisy-Vedrines   Barsac
Château Filhot   Sauternes
Château d'Arche   Sauternes

Château Broustet   Barsac
Château Caillou   Barsac
Château Suau   Barsac
Château de Malle   Preignac
Château Romer-Lafon   Fargues
Château Romer-de-la-Miremoy   Fargues
Château Lamothe   Sauternes
Château d'Arche-Lafaurie   Sauternes
Château Nairac   Barsac

Saint-Émilion

This vineyard, famed for its red wines, is situated about 30 kilometres to the east of Bordeaux, close to Libourne. It is on two very distinct types of soil: a clay and limestone plateau (Côtes de Saint-Émilion) and a sandy plain (Graves de Saint-Émilion) and produces high-class wines that are rich, full bodied and generous, and powerful enough to be compared to the wines of Burgundy. Merlot is used more than Cabernet in this area, and the ageing potential of the wine is as good as Médoc wines.

Eleven *crus* were classed *Premier Grand Cru* in 1958:

Château Ausone, the best known from the Côtes region
Château Cheval-Blanc, the most highly regarded from the Graves region
Château Figeac
Château Beauséjour (Dufau)
Château Beauséjour (Bécot)
Château Belair
Château Canon
Château La Gaffèliere-Naudes
Château Magdelaine
Château Pavie
Château Trottevieille
Clos Fourtet

Sixty-one earned the classification *Grand Cru*, among them the following:

Château Angelus
Château Bellevue
Château Canon-la-Gaffelière
Château Chauvin
Château Coutet
Château Curé-Bon
Château Fonplegade
Château Grand-Barrail-La-Marzelle
Château Grand-Corbin-Despagne
Château Grand-Pontet
Château Larcis-Ducasse
Château Latour-du-Pin-Figeac
Château Yon-Figeac
Château Ripeau
Château Troplong-Mondot

There are very few whites from this vineyard area.

There are five satellite villages around Saint-Émilion which produce some very respectable but less high-class red *crus*:

Saint-Georges
Puisseguin
Montagne
Lussac
Parsac

Pomerol

This vineyard is limited to the communes of Libourne and Pomerol. Only red wines are found here; they are exquisite, meaty, fat and high-calibre; popular, and deservedly so. There has never been an official classification, but the following are worth mentioning:

Château Pétrus, the best known
Château La Conseillante
Château L'Évangile
Château Gazin
Château Vieux-Certan
Château Trotanoy
Château Petit-Village
Clos L'Église
Château La Fleur
Château La Pointe
Château Nénin

Lalande-de-Pomerol and Néac

Come close to a Pomerol without being quite in the same class.

Bordeaux Côtes de Francs

Quality whites and reds produced in four villages to the east of Lussac-Saint-Émilion.

Bordeaux Côtes de Castillon

To the east of Libourne and on the right bank of the Dordogne there is a small vineyard that offers delightful and well balanced reds reminiscent of the Saint-Émilions.

Sainte-Foy-Bordeaux

Upstream of the Côtes de Castillon, the canton of Sainte-Foy-la-Grande and several neighbouring communes make up an area on the left bank producing dry and sweet whites with bouquet as well as some very pleasant reds.

Entre-Deux-Mers

This is all the land that lies between the Garonne and the Dordogne up to the Gironde estuary. It used to produce mainly sweet whites, but the vineyard was changed over early on, and now good dry whites are grown along with some reds, which are tending to take over from the whites. *Appellation contrôlée* is restricted to the dry whites; the sweet whites and reds are only able to claim *Bordeaux* or *Bordeaux supérieur*.

Bordeaux (Château Canon): Vats
(Photograph by J. P. Verney – Ministry of Agriculture archives)

Graves de Vayres
Two communes, Vayres and Arveyres, in the canton of Libourne, but in the Entre Deux Mers, produce sweet and dry whites and smooth reds with a bouquet which is not without a certain charm. The whites are the most common.

Les Premières Côtes de Bordeaux
These extend along the right bank of the Garonne upstream from Bordeaux to Cadillac. The sweet whites are excellent, Langoiran being well known. The reds are not without interest.

The name of the commune of origin may be added to the *appellation*.

Cadillac
Appellation that applies to the sweet whites from the southernmost areas of the Premières Côtes de Bordeaux.

Loupiac
Continues the Premières Côtes region southwards, producing only one type of wine; a sweet white that is full, creamy and with plenty of body.

Sainte-Croix-du-Mont
South of Loupiac on the right bank, opposite Sauternes. It is an excellent vineyard giving sweet white wines that are attractive and elegant, and have a soft milky smoothness. Château Loubens produces an equally distinguished dry white wine.

Côtes de Bordeaux-Sainte-Macaire
Situated more to the south and producing only whites.

Bordeaux-Haut-Benauge and Entre-Deux-Mers-Haut-Benauge
White wine *appellations* combining a small group of seven communes farther away from the banks of the Garonne than the previous ones, but nevertheless counted as being in the same district.

Fronsac
Extends the Libourne vineyards downstream along the Dordogne, westwards. It is a region of generous, solid and full bodied reds, comparable to the good *crus bourgeois* of Médoc.

Côtes de Canon-Fronsac
Combines some of the best individual parcels of land in Fronsac.

Bourg, Côtes de Bourg, Bourgeais
These *appellations* refer to the white and red wines of the canton of Bourg, on the right bank of the Gironde. The reds are full bodied and bright coloured, but sometimes lacking finesse.

Blaye or Blayais
This is the whole of the northern part of the department of Gironde, next to the estuary and facing Médoc. The wines are less high class and less well balanced, but it is possible to find the occasional small château producing a reasonably attractive red or white wine.

Premières Côtes de Blaye
The best wines from Blaye.

Côtes de Blaye
Appellation restricted to whites.

Vins de table

There are still numerous vineyards in Gironde making good *vins de table supérieurs*, mostly in Cubzac in the north, Coutras and Guitres to the north of Libourne, and Bazas in the south of the department. Their volume is significant because the producers have consented to declassification and designate approximately 30 per cent of the department's total harvest (of which two-thirds is white) to be used for *vins de consommation courante*, even though they may be from an *appellation contrôlée* area.

There are no *vins delimités de qualité supérieur* in Gironde and very few *vins de pays*.

The quality of these wines varies significantly depending on the growing location, the vine type, and how close it is to a high quality vineyard.

8

DORDOGNE

This vineyard, situated primarily along both banks of the Dordogne, runs adjacent to the east side of the Bordeaux vineyard.

The soil is varied, clay and limestone with a clay subsoil, but there are also some areas of sand and sandy-clay soils.

The vines planted are the same as in Gironde, with a few additions.

The *appellation d'origine contrôlée* wines account for approximately a third of the production, of which whites predominate over reds by 15–20 per cent.

There are no *vins delimités de qualité supérieure* in this area, nor *vins de pays*.

Appellations d'origine contrôlées

Bergerac
This *appellation* is reserved for the red, a neighbour of Bordeaux, but not as satisfying; its style is not unlike the *petits crus* of Gironde, but with less depth. The best of these earn the label *Côtes de Bergerac.*

Bergerac sec
The local producers put a lot of work into making this dry white wine. It is a close cousin of the best dry whites of Entre-deux-Mers and is very notable.

Côtes de Bergerac moelleux
Classifies the sweet whites which the region produces in great quantities. They are high in sugar, perfumed, generally less distinguished than those from Gironde.

The Côtes de Bergerac – Côtes de Saussignac
These are the product of four villages which are on the outskirts of the department of Sainte-Foy-la-Grande in the Dordogne.

Monbazillac
The prestigious *appellation* of the Dordogne. This small hilly area to the south of Bergerac comprises only five communes that produce white wines that are very sweet, creamy, and pleasantly smooth and rich. They lack only the finesse of the great sweet wines of Bordeaux.

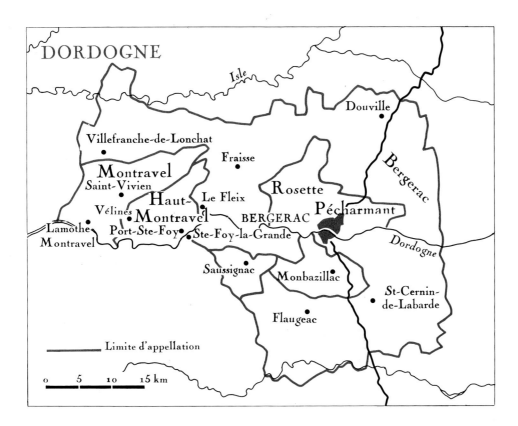

Montravel

This dry white wine has particular vigour and a distinctive taste of the soil, along with lots of character and attractiveness. The area of production is on the east bank of the Dordogne, between Bergerac and the border of Gironde, and is quite large. One or two very good cooperatives deserve a mention: Vélines, La-Mothe-Montravel, Saint-Vivien.

Côtes-de-Montravel and Haut-Montravel

These are the finest whites of the Montravel region, in the canton of Vélines. They are compulsorily sweet and are produced in smaller quantities than the dry wines.

Pécharmant

This is a red wine of the Bergerac region, quite light and pleasant and produced from the best Bordeaux vines.

Rosette

This is a small licensed area including Bergerac and five neighbouring communes. They produce a light bodied, delicate and elegant sweet white wine that comes from the same vines as the Sauternes of Gironde. The *vins de tables* from this department are fairly coarse. There are a few sweet white *vins primeurs* known as *vins de macadam* (tar wines)!

9

THE SOUTHWEST AND THE PYRENEES

THE SOUTHWEST

Between Bordeaux and the vast expanses of inland Languedoc, the vines are more sparsely and unevenly distributed.

A huge number of *vins ordinaires* are produced here, the departments of Lot-et-Garonne, Tarn-et-Garonne, Lot, Tarn, Aveyron and Haute-Garonne alone being home to almost 9 per cent of French winegrowers. However, *crus* of any interest are rare since the *appellation contrôlée* wines from these same departments represent only 1 per cent of the national total.

AVEYRON
Aveyron has three *vins delimités de qualité supérieure* rarely seen outside the locality:

- red, white and rosé wines from Entraygues et du Fel
- red, white and rosé wines from Estaing
- red and rosé wines from Marcillac.

LOT
Lot has the best *appellation d'origine contrôlée* of the region.

Cahors
This is exclusively red wine produced principally from the Cot or Malbec grape. It is sound, exceptionally robust and with great depth but can be rough, and all too often it does not have the finesse one would hope for. It has a distinctive bouquet and happily improves with age.

Lot produces two table wines.

- Vin des Coteaux de Glanes (from Bretenoux)
- Vin des Coteaux du Quercy which is produced in conjunction with Tarn-et-Garonne.

LOT-ET-GARONNE AND TARN-ET-GARONNE
The Lot-et-Garonne area borders Gironde to the west and can boast two good *appellation d'origine contrôlée* wines:

Côtes de Duras

There are twice as many sweet and dry white wines as reds, both produced from Bordeaux vines that give them a large part of their character.

Côtes de Buzet

Almost only reds are found in this area between Agen and Casteljaloux. They are well balanced, nervy and fruity wines that acquire a pleasant bouquet.

One *vin delimité de qualité supérieure* is produced here: *Côtes-du-Marmandais*: red, white and rosé.

Côtes-du-Brulhois is a *vin de pays* from Lot-et-Garonne and Tarn-et-Garonne.

Tarn-et-Garonne produces only one *vin delimité de qualité supérieure*: the white or red wine of Lavilledieu, to the west of Montauban; and it produces two *vins de pays*:

- *vin de pays de l'Agenais*, on the border of Lot-et-Garonne
- *vin de pays de Saint-Sardos*, in the south of the department.

TARN

Tarn has a good *appellation d'origine contrôlée* wine:

Gaillac

Produces slightly more white than red or rosé wines. The former are produced from Mauzac grapes. They are dry, quite forceful and with an attractive aroma that makes them delightful *vins primeurs*. These whites are often Perlé. The reds and rosés come from local, Gamay or Bordeaux vines, and can be of very good quality, full bodied, satisfying, and with an original nose.

- *Gaillac Premières Côtes* is a selection from the best communes and must have a higher alcohol content.
- *Gaillac doux* (white) has a fairly high level of non-fermented sugar. It is extremely enjoyable while still very young.
- *Gaillac mousseux* has an original and pronounced taste, and is made by completing the fermentation in bottles rather than adding more sugar.

The *vin de pays des Côtes du Tarn* is produced in most of the department.

HAUTE-GARONNE

Haute-Garonne, together with Tarn-et-Garonne, makes an *appellation d'origine contrôlée* wine:

Côtes-du-Frontonais

Red and rosé only, produced mostly from an unusual grape type, the Negrette. The *appellation* may be followed by either of two qualifications: Fronton or Villaudric, depending on where it was produced. These wines have a pronounced character, are firm but quite light, and are mostly enjoyed by their local followers.

GERS

This department does not make great wines, but it does produce an *eau-de-vie* – spirit – that is very well known.

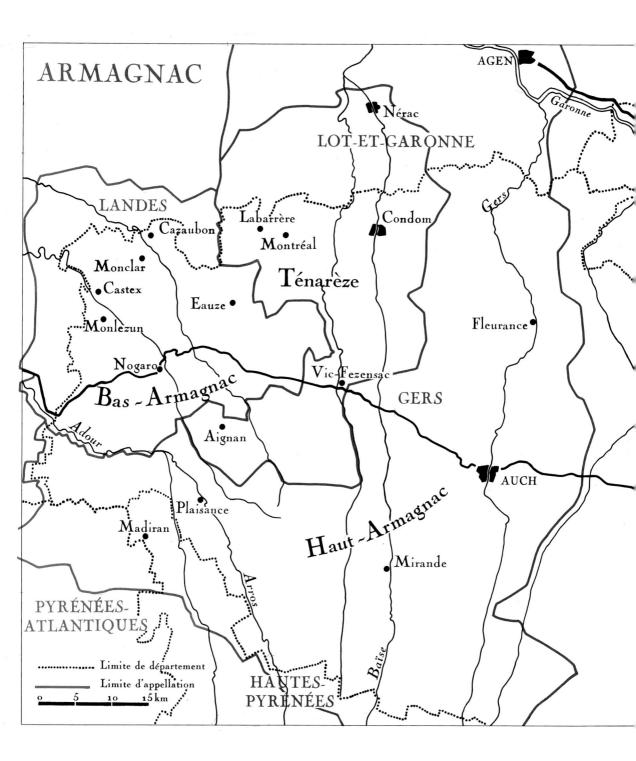

Armagnac

On soil which varies between the sandstone of the lowlands to the limestone hills, several different grape varieties are grown, the most important being the Piquepoul. (Piquepoul is the local name for Folle Blanche.) This makes a sharp wine that is rather rough, but able to produce very good alcohol. The wine is distilled using a disc machine of a certain regulated type, something between a pot-still and a continuous still.

Armagnac is characterised by its violet-like flavour, which becomes more pronounced after ageing in casks or barrels, and its delicate and subtle scent.

Bas-Armagnac is the better brandy, especially when it comes from the so-called 'Grand Bas' regions of Castex, Monclar, Monlezun and, most of all, from the 'Fin Bas' region of Cazaubon.

Ténarèze is the *appellation* used by the following regions: Eauze (Grandes Ténarèzes), Labarrère and Montréal (Petites Ténarèzes).

Haut-Armagnac is produced in Condom and Vic-Fézensac.

Vin de Pays

One or two smaller wines claim a regional *appellation*:

- *vin de pays des Côtes de Gascogne*: from the whole department
- *vin de pays des Côtes du Condomois*
- *vin de pays des Côtes de Montestruc*
- *vin de pays des Côtes de Saint-Mont*.

THE UPPER AND ATLANTIC PYRENEES

The valley slopes here are the home of an original vineyard. (The East Pyrenees are counted as part of inland Languedoc.)

Appellations d'origine contrôlées

Jurançon (ATLANTIC PYRENEES)

This wine was made famous by Henri IV. It is produced from local grape types, the Manseng and the Courbu. It is a sweet white wine, with lots of nose, very attractive and cheeky but having a certain finesse and a capacity to age very well indeed, producing wines with a marvellous bouquet. Owners in this area are now inclining more to the production of a dry white wine, possessing the same qualities as the sweet, but without its ageing potential.

Madiran

Produced largely from a local vine type, the Tannat, this distinctive red wine is purplish, tannic and harsh when young, but after at least a year in the barrel and the bottle it becomes fragrant, round and satisfying. It is a good example of a bouquet wine.

It is cultivated over a large area covering part of the Atlantic Pyrenees and part of the Upper Pyrenees.

Pacherenc-du-Vic-Bilh

This is the white from the same region. It is generally dry, flavourful, has a distinctive style and sometimes develops an attractive bouquet. It is made from Ruffiac (also called Pacherenc) grapes.

Irouléguy (ATLANTIC PYRENEES)

This wine is the *vin de pays* of Basque. The rosé is the favourite: light and smooth, with an attractive aroma and capable of acquiring a pleasant bouquet.

Béarn

Produced in both departments, its quality varies tremendously depending on the area of production. The rosé is generally smooth and fruity; the white is dry, fragrant and not at all harsh; the red is often somewhat unresolved but improves in quality by being kept for a little while.

Vin delimité de qualité supérieure

Tursan (Landes) is harvested in the region to the south of Mont-de-Marsan, between the River Adour and the departmental border.

The red is purplish and firm, reminiscent of, though less refined than, a Bordeaux wine. There are also rosés and dry whites, their quality being extremely variable.

Vins de table

These are mostly whites and are very common in the department of Landes, but more often than not they are rough and with a distinct taste of the soil. They have no ageing potential whatsoever. The most productive areas are Chalosse to the east of Dax and 'Sables' on the bay of Gascogne.

10
LES CHARENTES

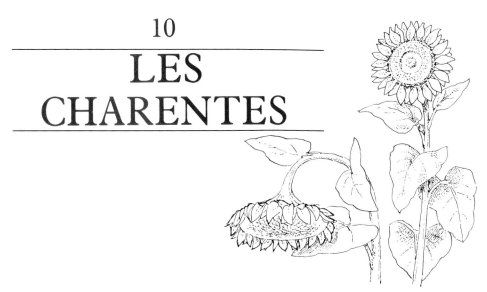

The two departments of la Charente and la Charente-Maritime are the proud owners of an extensive vineyard, their total wine production being more than that of Aude, and approaching that of Herault. They therefore play a very important role in French viticulture. But most of the wine is not consumed in its natural state. It is destined for the distillery, to be turned into the best spirit in the world: Cognac. The wine which is not distilled is sold as dry white *vin ordinaire.*

The white wine produced from the Charentes vines is in fact unattractive. Folle Blanche, Saint-Émilion (the local name for white Ugni), Colombard and a few other grapes are suited to producing neither aromatic wines, nor bouquet wines, but strangely enough produce a spirit that has the potential of acquiring exceptional qualities, given enough time. Nature has its paradoxes.

The Charentes soil is mostly limestone, and although the leaves of the vines do tend to turn yellow, in general the best *crus* are found where the chalk is most abundant and appears on top of the arable land, giving the countryside an appearance similar to that of Champagne.

To make the Cognac, a single-heater pot-still called a *charentais* is used whose operation is rigorously defined by law. Each heating produces a *brouilli* (alcohol which has vapourised and then condensed). The combined *brouillis* are then redistilled; this second distillation is called *la bonne chauffe.* The first and last fractions of the distillation, the 'head' and 'tail', are discarded, and what remains – the 'heart' – is Cognac.

The *appellation d'origine contrôlée* Cognac or Eau-de-Vie de Cognac has been regulated since 1936 and may be used by the whole area that is defined by law, which can be subdivided into almost concentric zones:

• Grande Champagne or Grande Fine Champagne has Segonzac as its centre and extends as far as the town of Cognac. This area makes the best *eaux-de-vie*; they are the most delicate, highest class and have the most length.
• Petite Champagne or Petite Fine Champagne almost totally surrounds the previous area, and contains Barbezieux, Archiac and Châteauneuf. Their *eaux-de-vie* have great verve and an excellent flavour.

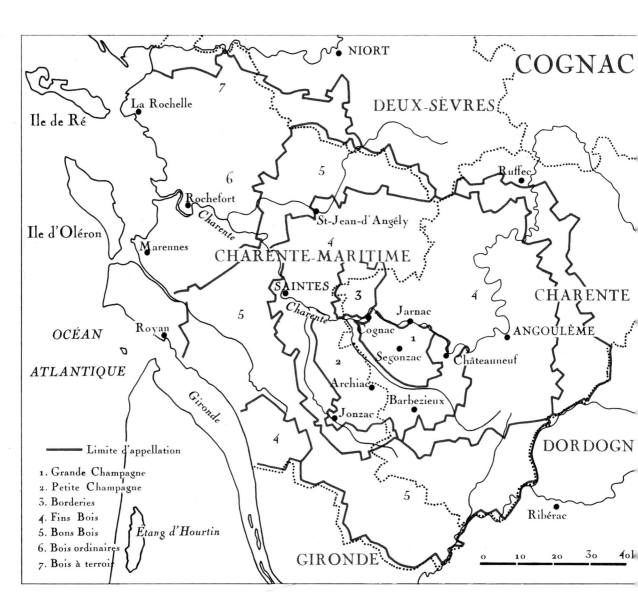

NIORT

COGNAC

DEUX-SÈVRES

Ile de Ré

La Rochelle

7

Ruffec

6

5

Rochefort

Charente

St-Jean-d'Angély

Ile d'Oléron

Marennes

4

CHARENTE-MARITIME

SAINTES

CHARENTE

3

4

Charente

Jarnac

ANGOULÊME

OCÉAN

Royan

5

Cognac

1

ATLANTIQUE

Segonzac

Châteauneuf

Gironde

2

Archiac

Barbezieux

Jonzac

DORDOGN

——— Limite d'appellation

1. Grande Champagne
2. Petite Champagne
3. Borderies
4. Fins Bois
5. Bons Bois
6. Bois ordinaires
7. Bois à terroir

Étang d'Hourtin

4

5

Ribérac

GIRONDE

0   10   20   3o   4o

- Fine Champagne is made by combining the above two *eaux-de-vie*.
- Borderies is a very small area to the west of Cognac.
- Fins Bois is a huge area that totally surrounds the first three areas and spills over into Charente-Maritime as far as Saintes and reaching past Angoulême in the west.
- Bons Bois surround the Fins Bois area and spread out in every direction. Les Bois Ordinaires extend towards the sea as far as Rochefort and Royan. Les Bois *à terroir* or Bois *communs* stretch as far as the coast to include the islands of Ré and Oléron.

Cognac has to be aged in traditional oak casks for a certain length of time to have the right to use the following labels:

*** : After two or three years of ageing

V.O. (Very Old)
V.S.O.P. (Very Superior Old Pale) } after four years
Réserve

Extra, Napoléon, Vieille Réserve } after five years
Hors d'Age

But really great *eaux-de-vie* can be kept much longer than this, providing the producer is willing to accept the considerable losses caused by evaporation from the casks.

The *appellation* Eau-de-Vie des Charentes may also be used.

L'Ésprit de Cognac is an *eau-de-vie* that is 80–85° proof and is used to make *liqueurs de dosage* that are added to Champagne and other sparkling wines.

Le Pineau de Charentes is a dessert wine obtained by adding Cognac that has been left to go sour to a must of local grapes.

11

BURGUNDY

GROWING CONDITIONS

The Chablis vineyard comprises twenty or so communes on both banks of the Serein, halfway between Auxerre and Tonerre. It is on limestone hills planted with a single variety of vine, the white Chardonnay. The huge vineyard of upper Burgundy is on the slopes of the wide Sâone valley. This ridge is about 60 kilometres long, from Dijon to Chagny, and its width varies considerably between 650 and 3500 metres. The soil is mostly oolitic limestone, mixed with marl to a greater or lesser extent, on a bedrock of thin schist. Only one grape type, Pinot, is authorised for the very best *appellation d'origine contrôlée* reds; and, similarly, Chardonnay is the only grape type authorised for whites.

The Burgundy climate is more or less continental with its hot summers that often last well into the harvest, but there are harsh winters and late springs that bring frosts to the first buds. Chablis has cruelly suffered from this, but the recent installation of heaters among the vines has drastically reduced losses.

THE *CRUS*

Appellations d'origine contrôlées

Nowadays, these account for two-thirds of the production of the department of Yonne (Chablis vineyard), and almost all of the Côte d'Or.

The principal villages of the Burgundy coast now have the right to add the principal *cru* of the area to their name. Thus Chambolle becomes Chambolle-Musigny. But beware: every Chambolle is not a Musigny – far from it! In fact, this *cru* represents only a very small part of the wine of Chambolle, but it is the most valuable and prestigious part.

The name of the specific *climat* (field) may also be added to the name of the village; for example, Chambolle-Musigny-les-Charmes; and finally, this may be replaced by the words *Premier Cru* if the area has been given approval by the Committee of Experts.

BURGUNDY

Apart from covering Yonne and the Côte d'Or, this *appellation* also includes Saône-et-Loire and the Villefranche district in the Rhône department. Grapes other than Pinot are allowed in red wines, such as the white-juiced Gamay Noir, and in white wines grapes other than the Chardonnay are authorised, among them Pinot Blanc.

It is difficult to generalise about all the wines that appear under the Burgundy label. They are usually quite powerful, but are of variable finesse and fullness.

Towards the northern limits of the wine growing area there are some years when the fruit does not manage to mature properly, and it is very often necessary to augment the natural sugars in the must with ordinary sugar, so as to obtain a high enough alcohol content. Thus a certain alcoholic strength is maintained, with or without the addition of sugar (chaptalisation). But although warm years produce wines that are full, opulent, satisfying and very refined, or even of exceptional breed, bad years result in wines that are thin and hollow, where only the augmentation of alcohol can give them the desired depth and fullness. Another problem is the late rains that tend to rot the grapes, especially Pinot grapes, which are clustered closely together like a pine cone (hence the name).

Winegrowing is more risky in Burgundy than in Bordeaux, and this explains the high prices for which Burgundy producers are often criticised.

In a good year, red Burgundies are just as good as those of Bordeaux. They have an exceptional warmth, fleshiness and fullness, and with time develop wonderful round, expansive bouquets that give them a unique brilliance.

The white wines of Burgundy are all dry wines that age well, and have an elegance, charm and frankness that give them the well deserved reputation of being the best in the world.

The volume of production in Burgundy is much lower than in Bordeaux; the area of vines in the Côte d'Or only accounts for 8 per cent of the Gironde, and the yield per hectare is generally lower. This is another reason for the discrepancy in prices.

Bourgogne clairet or *rosé* is not very common. The area of Dijon, which was the principal producer, has now been absorbed into the suburbs of the town, but there are still one or two estates dotted along the coast.

Bourgogne ordinaire and *Bourgogne grand ordinaire* designate wines with the lowest alcoholic strength. The rosés are called *Bourgogne ordinaire rosé* or *clairet*, and *Bourgogne grand ordinaire rosé* or *clairet*.

Bourgogne passe-tout-grain is a blend of wine from Pinot grapes (at least a third) and wine from white-juiced Pinot Noir. It is lighter and has less substance than the Burgundy made from Pinot alone, but its aroma makes it attractive when young. It is not really suited to being laid down.

Bourgogne Aligoté is the name given to a white wine made from Aligoté grapes; it is less refined than the Chardonnay, which may sometimes be blended with it. The commune of Bouzeron (in Saône et Loire) may add its name to the *appellation*.

Bourgogne mousseux is produced by a secondary fermentation in bottles by the champagne method. It is often a good quality wine.

Le crémant de Bourgogne is one degree lower in alcohol and is less effervescent.

CHABLIS

This dry white wine has attained worldwide renown. A large proportion of the wine produced goes for export, and this has a considerable effect on its price. It is a wine with some exceptional qualities: it has a particularly attractive green colour, a subtle nose, incomparable lightness and exquisite delicacy. It is among the world's finest dry white wines. Moreover, it has the advantage of being delightful when young, but also ageing well and developing an excellent bouquet.

Chablis Grand Cru

These are the vineyard's highest calibre wines:

Les Vaudésirs
Les Preuses
Valmur
Les Grenouille
Les Clos
Les Blanchots
Les Bougros

Chablis Premier Cru

Although these wines are classed below the *grands crus*, they deserve to stand out from the crowd. The best include:

La Fourchaume
Le Mont-de-Milieu
Les Vaillons
Les Montmains
La Montée-de-Tonnerre

Burgundy: Le Clos Vougeot
(Photograph by J. P. Verney – Ministry of Agriculture archives)

Chablis
The majority of the wine made in the region is bottled as Chablis *tout court*.

Petit Chablis
Somewhat lighter and less distinguished, nevertheless fruity and nervy. The *appellation* may be completed by the addition of the name of the commune of origin.

Bourgogne Irancy
These red, rosé and *clairet* wines, produced solely from the commune of Irancy in the south of Auxerre, benefit from an *appellation contrôlée* classification. They are attractive wines, and not without charm in a good year.

LA GRANDE CÔTE BOURGIGNONNE
This vast vineyard runs southwards from Dijon, starting in the outskirts of the

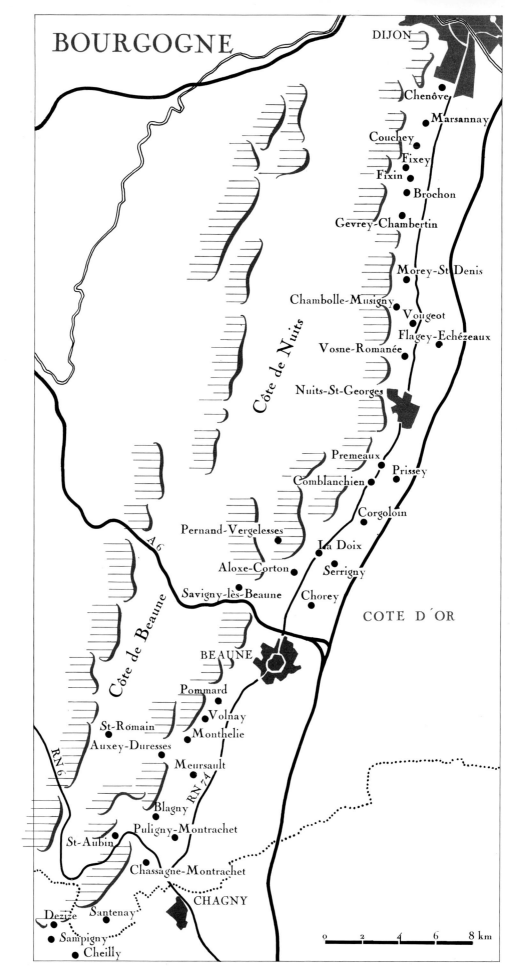

BOURGOGNE

DIJON

Chenôve

Marsannay

Couchey

Fixey

Fixin

Brochon

Gevrey-Chambertin

Morey-St-Denis

Chambolle-Musigny

Vougeot

Flagey-Echézeaux

Vosne-Romanée

Côte de Nuits

Nuits-St-Georges

Premeaux

Prissey

Comblanchien

Corgoloin

Pernand-Vergelesses

La Doix

Aloxe-Corton

Serrigny

A 6

Savigny-lès-Beaune

Chorey

COTE D´OR

Côte de Beaune

BEAUNE

Pommard

Volnay

St-Romain

Monthelie

Auxey-Duresses

RN 6

Meursault

RN 74

Blagny

Puligny-Montrachet

St-Aubin

Chassagne-Montrachet

CHAGNY

Dezize

Santenay

Sampigny

Cheilly

0   2   4   6   8 km

town itself. The northern tip, whose area is gradually being eaten away by urban development is:

Bourgogne-Marsannay-la-Côte

This commune's reputation came mostly from its fresh, fragrant rosés, which are very rarely made now. They have a special *appellation*: *Bourgogne clairet* (or *rosé) Marsannay-la-Côte.*

The *Grands Crus* are split up into two separate areas, the dividing line being at the village of Comblanchien. In the north there is the Côte de Nuits, and in the south, the Côte de Beaune. In both regions villages produce their best *crus* from the wonderful southeast-facing slopes, between the plain, which usually produces rough wines, and the top of the hill.

LA CÔTE DE NUITS

Almost entirely red wines are produced here. They are fuller bodied, sturdier and meatier than those of the Côte de Beaune. They develop more slowly but attain quite exceptional class and power, mostly due to their striking bouquet. Great names from the royal family of wine are to be found here.

Fixin

This is the northernmost village, producing wines that are not totally without interest, but are overshadowed by the prestigious *crus* being produced to the south.

Gevrey-Chambertin

Nervy, full bodied, vigorous and very sappy. Exceptional *crus*:

Chambertin
Clos de Bèze.

Other notable *crus*:

Latricières-Chambertin
Mazoyères-Chambertin
Charmes-Chambertin
Mazis-Chambertin
Griottes-Chambertin
Ruchottes-Chambertin
Chapelle-Chambertin
Clos-Saint-Jaques
Les Ruchottes.

Morey-Saint-Denis

Comparable to Gevrey-Chambertin, solid and full bodied. Notable *crus*:

Clos de Tart
Clos Saint-Denis
Clos de la Roche
Clos des Lambrays.

Chambolle-Musigny

The most delicate and the most refined of the Côte de Nuits wines, it has a big bouquet and great distinction. Exceptional *crus*:

Musigny
Bonnes-Mares.

Other notable *crus*:

Les Amoureuses
Les Charmes.

Vougeot

Elegant, full bodied, but smooth and silky. Exceptional *cru*: Le Clos Vougeot.

Flagey-Echezeaux

Only the Echezeaux and Grands Echezeaux *crus* have an *appellation contrôlée*. These are full, nervy and very delicate wines. Some of the commune is on flat land.

Vosne-Romanée

A satisfying, very round wine that is less solid than a Gevrey and fuller bodied than a Chambolle; very distinctive. Exceptional *crus*:

Romanée-Conti
Romanée-Saint-Vivant
La Romanée
La Tâche
Richebourg.

Other notable *crus*:

Les Malconsorts
Les Suchots
Les Beaux Monts.

Nuits-Saint-Georges or Nuits

Satisfying, fat and robust, these wines are a little less refined than a Chambolle or Vosne. Principal *crus*:

Les Saint-Georges
Les Cras
Les Pruliers
Les Boudots
Les Vaucrains.

To complete the list of Côte de Nuits wines, there are the *vins primeurs*:

Clos de la Maréchale
Les Corvées.

Vins fins de la Côte de Nuits and Côtes de Nuit-Villages

These two *appellations* apply to the villages of Fixin and Brochon in the north and Corgoloin, Comblanchien and Prissey in the south.

Burgundy: The wine press at Clos Vougeot
(Photograph by Pierre Mackiewicz – Institut Technique du Vin)

Le Bourgogne – Vin fin des hautes Côtes de Nuits

This is produced in several communes that are not actually on the *côte*, but on the so-called *arrière côte*, to the west of the *grands crus*. A few pleasant wines can be found here, but they cannot compare with the quality of those listed above.

There are one or two *clairets* or rosés; *Bourgogne clairet* (or *rosé*), *Vin fin des hautes Côtes de Nuits*.

LA CÔTE DE BEAUNE

The northern half of this region produces mainly red wines, while white wines predominate in the south. The reds are softer and less forceful than those of the Côte de Nuits, and they have smoothness, grace and an altogether more feminine elegance. Their colour is often less intense than that of their neighbours, whose quality they cannot really match. They definitely make up an inferior branch of the noble Burgundy family.

Pernand-Vergelesses

Produces some very distinctive reds (*cru* Les Vergelesses) and some noteworthy, delicate-nosed whites (*cru* En-Charlemagne).

Aloxe Corton

The red is round and smooth, but also very nervy, strong and distinguished. The principal *crus* are:

Corton
Corton Clos de Roi
Corton-Bressandes
Les Charmes
Les Renards.

There are also some great dry whites with incredible delicacy, breed, and brilliance.

Corton blanc
Corton-Charlemagne.

Savigny-lès-Beaune

Produces only red wine which is nervy and lighter, but of good quality in a good year. It has a characteristic redcurrant flavour. One vineyard well worth mentioning is Les Lavières.

Ladoix-Serrigny

Also produces some interesting *crus*, such as Vergennes.

Beaune

The reds are by far the most significant here, and their incredible finesse, their classy style and their roundness place them among the top wines of the Côte d'Or. Their colour is often quite soft and with time acquires extremely attractive orange tones. The principal *crus* are:

Les Marconnets
Les Grèves
Les Fèves
Les Champimonts
Les Cras
Le Clos des Mouches
Le Clos du Roi
Les Bressandes.

The famous Hospices of Beaune which own vines along the whole of the Côte have achieved international fame by auctioning their harvest every year in November.

Chorey-lès-Beaune

Pleasant but less refined than Beaune.

Pommard

Produces only reds. They are rich, solid and full wines with a good strong body and toughness, but their finesse suffers occasionally from their excessive sturdiness.

Les Epenots ⎫
Les Argillières ⎬ fairly light wines
Les Rugiens ⎭
Les Arvelets
Les Bertins
La Chanière
Les Boucherottes
La Commaraine

Volnay

Again, only a red wine is produced, and this is the lightest, most distinguished and most elegantly refined of the Côte de Beaune wines. It can however lack depth in a less good year.

Les Caillerets (the most famous *cru*)
Les Champans
Bousse d'Or
Les Chevrets
Les Mitans
L'Ormeau
Les Angles
Les Fremiets
Le Clos des Chênes.

Volnay Santenots

A classy and distinguished growth produced in the commune of Meursault.

Monthélie

Full bodied reds. They take time to develop but positively bloom after long enough in the bottle. Very few whites are found.

Auxey-Duresses

Wines similar to Monthélie. The principal *cru* is Les Duresses. Whites account for a third of production.

Meursault

This is where the great *Côte des blancs* begins. The dry white wine produced here is round, refined, extremely delicate and has a striking bouquet. The principal *crus* are:

Les Perrières
Les Charmes
Les Genevrières
Les Poruzots
Goutte-d'Or
Les Tessons
Les Bouchères.

Blagny

A hamlet sitting on the border of Meursault and Puligny; it has its own *appellation* but only for reds. The whites are called Meursault-Blagny.

Puligny-Montrachet

This is the top-class white Burgundy. Its incredible finesse, its charm and its delicate and attractive bouquet make it one of the greatest white wines in the world, if not the greatest.

Le Montrachet (the most rounded)
Le Chevalier-Montrachet (very delicate)
Le Bâtard-Montrachet (a little more solid)
Les Bienvenues-Bâtard-Montrachet
Les Combettes
Le Cailleret
Les Chalumeaux
Les Folatières.

Chassagne-Montrachet

Also a high-class wine but with more body and fullness than the Puligny, and this solidity can detract from its elegance in a heavy year. There are also some good quality reds under this *appellation*.

Montrachet, Chevalier-Montrachet and Bâtard-Montrachet overlap into the two communes of Puligny and Chassagne.

Another noteworthy white *cru* exclusively in the commune of Chassagne is *Les Criots-Bâtard-Montrachet*.

Santenay

This is a noteworthy red vineyard at the southern tip of the Côte d'Or. Whites are practically non-existent. Santenay reds are medium bodied, nervy and develop a very good nose but do not reach the same standard of finesse as the great wines of the Côte. Worth mentioning are:

Les Gravières
Le Clos de Tavannes.

Dezizes-lès-Maranges, Cheilly-lès-Maranges, Sampigny-lès-Maranges

These vineyards extend the Côte into the department of Saône-et-Loire. Their red wines make up most of the *appellation Côtes de Beaune-Villages*, and are usually sold under that name.

Côtes de Beaune

This *appellation* groups together all the wines, which are mostly red, that are produced on the Côte de Beaune, and the commune of origin may precede it. In general they are fairly light and pleasant wines; they do not attain exceptional quality, but are very drinkable.

Côtes de Beaune-Villages

Wine with this *appellation* comes from one or more villages which have a right to use it.

Bourgogne des Hautes Côtes de Beaune

This *appellation* applies to 20 or so communes on the *arrière-côte*, to the south of the Hautes Côtes de Nuits and to the west of the Grande Côte. A variety of wines are produced here, often quite drinkable; respectable but unassuming.

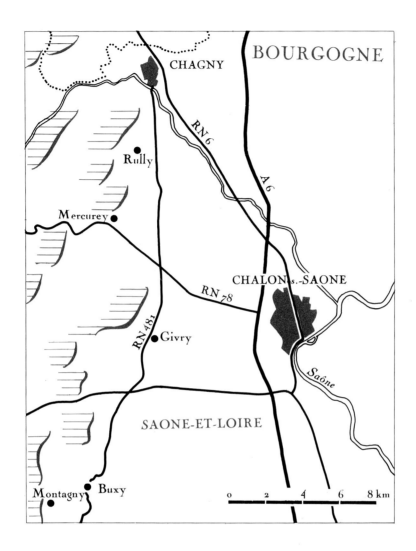

Saint-Romain

This is one of the *arrière-côte*'s best *crus* and deserves a special mention. Slightly more whites than reds are found here.

Saint-Aubin

Further south and close to Chagny, this is also part of the *arrière-côte*. Reds predominate over whites. Both are often of equal quality with those of the heartland of the Grande Côte.

LA CÔTE CHALONNAISE

This is the extension of the great vineyard of the Côte d'Or into the department of Saône-et-Loire. It is possible to find good red and white *crus* here which, although lacking the fullness, smoothness and finesse of a Côte de Beaune or a Nuits, nevertheless have a good nose, attractiveness and a certain lightness that give them charm. They also have the advantage of developing more quickly.

Mercurey

The reds, which are far more important than the whites, are delicate, nervy, and have a good bouquet.

Rully

To the south of Chagny, Rully produces as much white wine as red, but both in small quantities. The reds are more solid and less inspiring than the Mercureys.

Givry

Near Chalon-sur-Saône, Givry produces mostly light, elegant reds with a pleasant bouquet.

Montagny

Exclusively white wines from Chardonnay grapes in four villages in the Buxy region.

Vins délimités de qualité superieure

There is only one in Basse-Bourgogne (Lower Burgundy): Sauvignon de Saint-Bris, an aromatic wine that is crisp and clean but quite full, produced in the Irancy region.

Vins de table

Avallonnais, and the regions of Sens, Joigny, Tonnerois and Auxerrois all produce both red and white wines that are light and lively. In bad years they become thin and acid.

The Côte Chalonnaise extends southwards towards Mâcon in the form of a huge, quite sparse vineyard where it is nevertheless possible to find one or two little light and cheeky wines. The whites are most common in the localities of Saint-Gengoux and Sennecey-le-Grand, up to the border of the Mâcon district where the *zone delimitée* of Mâconnais whites begins.

12

MÂCONNAIS BEAUJOLAIS LYONNAIS

This huge vineyard lies between Burgundy and the Côtes du Rhône. Like Burgundy, it runs along the Saône valley, but following the river more closely. It is quite wide, stretching several kilometres to the west.

The border between the departments of Saône-et-Loire and Rhône is said to separate Mâconnais from Beaujolais. The viticultural area of Lyonnais begins in the Arbresle region and extends down to the southern border of the department of Rhône, across from Vienne on the other bank of the Rhône.

GROWING CONDITIONS

The land in Mâconnais is mostly limestone. Beaujolais is more varied: granite, schist, clay and limestone. In this vast area the gentle slopes, from the high lands of Charolais in the west down to the Saône valley, are marked out with ridges on which the vines grow.

The climate is hotter than in Burgundy, although the winters are hard and the spring frosts dangerous. The vast Saône–Rhône corridor can be the scene of violent storms which all too often result in destroyed crops. The rotting of the grapes which may occur at the end of the season is feared here as much as it is in Burgundy.

The most widespread vines are Gamay for reds and Chardonnay for whites. However, some *appellations* are allowed to add Pinot Noir to their reds and Aligoté to their whites. The yield per hectare is significantly higher than in Burgundy, the harvest from Beaujolais and Beaujolais-Villages reaching 800,000 hectolitres in a good year. The Mâcon reds and whites together come to scarcely 150,000 hectolitres.

THE *CRUS*

Appellations d'origine contrôlées

These represent approximately 50 per cent of the Saône-et-Loire production, and 90 per cent of the Rhône.

MÂCONNAIS
This region produces red wines that are pleasant and fruity, and high quality

whites. All the Mâconnais and Beaujolais *appellations* may be followed by the name of the locality of origin, providing the wine meets the minimum standards.

Mâcon (RED OR ROSÉ)

This *appellation* applies to wines produced in the Mâcon *arrondissement* (district), from authorised grape types and under specific conditions. It is a wine that is usually light, frivolous and cheeky and should be drunk young.

Mâcon (WHITE) or Pinot-Chardonnay-Mâcon

From the excellent Chardonnay grape come these delicious wines that are of higher quality than the reds. Fruity, lively and bright, they can be kept for several years.

Mâcon supérieur (RED AND WHITE)

Must be at least 11°.

Mâcon-Villages (WHITE)

The *appellation* is reserved for a group of communes situated in the south of the Mâcon blanc *appellation* zone. The following villages are worth mentioning: Viré, Clessé, Lugny, Azé, Igé, Verzé, Saint-Gengoux-de-Scissé and Prissé.

Pouilly-Fuissé

This small vineyard of only four communes (Fuissé and Solutré in the hamlet of Pouilly, Vergisson and Chaintré), produces a particularly distinguished, well bred and elegant wine, comparable in class to a Chablis.

Pouilly-Vinzelles and Pouilly-Loché

Appellation reserved for these two communes that are adjacent to Pouilly-Fuissé.

Saint-Vérand

The *appellation* applies to seven communes that produce a dry white wine comparable to the preceding *appellation*.

BEAUJOLAIS

This huge wine producing area, which is about 50 kilometres long and 15 wide, is divided into two by the Nizerand, a small river that enters the Saône a little downstream from Villefranche. The part that lies to the north of this river is known as *haut* Beaujolais, and the part to the south is known as *bas* Beaujolais or Beaujolais *bâtard*. Most of the Beaujolais villages are in *haut* Beaujolais.

Beaujolais

This generic *appellation* covers the production of the whole area. Beaujolais red wine is certainly the most popular in France. It is an aromatic wine, very fruity and with a real smell of fresh grapes, clean, quite light and cheeky. It is a happy wine that can very well be drunk as a new wine, and does not keep for very long. Unfortunately, vintages vary a lot. If the sun has been miserly, Beaujolais wine reflects this, and a great deal of its charm is missing. In a sunny year the wine will have the panache and the fruity flavour that can only be found in a good Beaujolais.

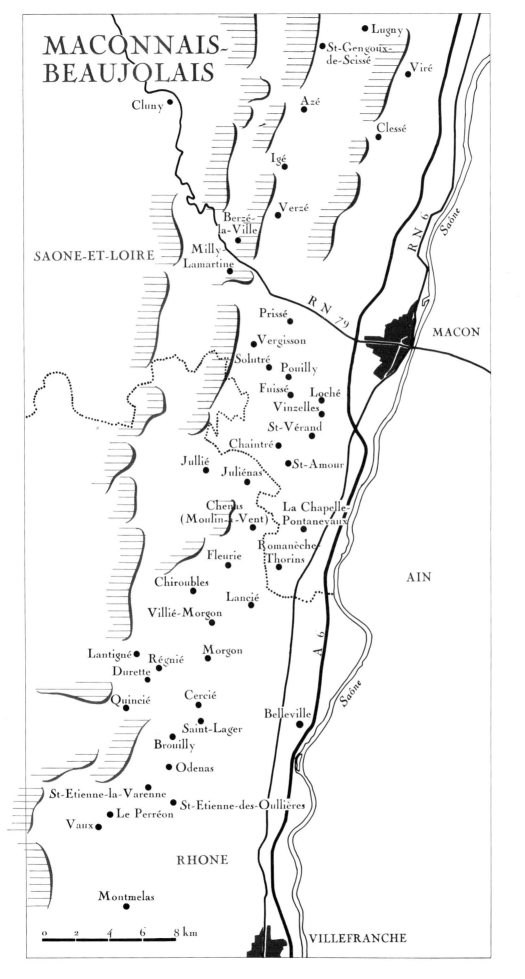

Beaujolais supérieure
This must have a higher alcohol content.

Beaujolais blanc
This *appellation* is very successful. The wine is made from Chardonnay grapes grown in the area near the border of Saône-et-Loire and Rhône. It is delicate and easy-going, very close to a Saint-Véran or the best Mâcon blanc; it is even allowed to use the Mâcon blanc *appellation*.

Beaujolais-Villages
These, the best holdings in Beaujolais, are in the northern part of the defined area. They are meatier, fuller bodied, and have a particularly attractive fruitiness and aroma. The following are worth mentioning: Montmelas, Vaux, Le Perréon, Saint-Étienne-la-Varenne, Saint-Étienne-des-Oullières, Quincié, Lantigné, Regnié, Lancié, Cercié, Durette and there are many more.

The region known as *crus* begins immediately to the south of the white Mâcon vineyard, and is the northernmost part of the Beaujolais area. The villages are spread out, running from north to south, on tall hills which have very good exposure; they all produce only red wine.

Saint-Amour
This is a *cru* of the Beaujolais vineyard, and produces only reds from Gamay vines. They are quite light bodied wines with a flowery aroma, and have great charm while still young.

Moulin-à-Vent
Only red wine is produced here, the sturdiest and most satisfying wine from the *cru* region of Beaujolais. Possessing a powerful aroma, solidity and a generous character, it reaches its full potential after a laying-down period which is quite short, but very necessary. As with the *grands crus* of Beaujolais, this is an exception to the rule that Gamay wines do not age well. However, it should not be kept for more than three to four years.

The *cru* is produced partly in the commune of Romanèche-Thorins (called l'En Haut), in the department of Saône-et-Loire, and partly in Chenas in the department of Rhône.

Juliénas
Adjacent to Saint-Amour, at the edge of Saône-et-Loire. The *cru* is exclusively red and characterised by its deep colour, its nerve and its fullness. It is one of the most well rounded of the Beaujolais wines. Its youthful harshness demands a little ageing in the bottle; only after one or two years does it reach its potential brilliance.

Chenas
Also red, this neighbour of Moulin-à-Vent is strong and robust; in fact this village contributes to the production of Moulin-à-Vent. The *appellation* extends to part of the commune of la Chapelle-Pontatevaux.

Fleurie
This is a more velvety and more elegant red wine, with a lightness which does not however hide a rich and powerful depth. Its pleasant grapiness and original style make it one of the most attractive Beaujolais wines.

Chiroubles

This red wine comes from the vineyards at the highest altitude, and is often affected by spring frosts. It is a full bodied, powerful wine, bigger than the Fleurie and more heady.

Morgon

This red wine is produced in Villié-Morgon on an area of schist where the ground is described as *terre pourrie* (rotten) or *terre à morgon*. It has a very distinctive and very pleasant character. It is solid and robust and will keep for quite a long time.

Brouilly

This exclusively red wine is grown around the mountain of the same name. It is meaty, somewhat nervy and very flavourful, with vigorous sappiness. It does not have the finesse of a Morgon or a Fleurie.

Côte de Brouilly

This *appellation* groups together the best *climats* (individual fields) in Brouilly, including Odenas, Saint-Lager, Cercié and Quincié.

COTEAUX DU LYONNAIS

In the south of the Beaujolais area there is an area spreading westwards from Lyon where the vine is more sparse, but where some fresh, fruity, medium bodied, but somewhat hollow red wines are made from the Gamay grape. Whites are made from the Chardonnay, Aligoté, and Melon (called Gamay Blanc); this area is the Coteaux du Lyonnais, and their defined area includes 60 or so villages. The main centre is in Saint-Bel. This region was elevated from V.D.Q.S. TO A.O.C. in 1984.

Vins de table

There are quite a few on the Mâconnais and Lyonnais ridges, but they are rare in Beaujolais. Their quality is variable, but usually they are quite light. Generally, anything of a certain class is able to benefit from an *appellation*.

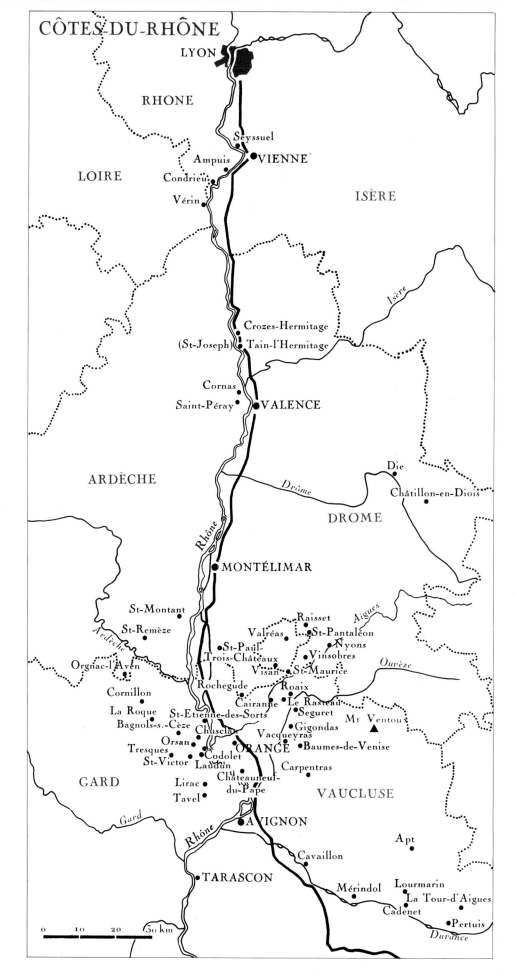

13

THE CÔTES DU RHÔNE

This large wine growing region runs along either side of the Rhône from Lyon to Avignon. It is about 12 km wide on the left bank and up to 20 km on the right.

It can be divided into two unequal parts: the first runs from Vienne at the mouth of the Drôme and the other from Donzère at the mouth of the Durance. Between these two boundaries there is an area of 40 km or so, where few vines are grown.

GROWING CONDITIONS

In the north the soil is light and dry crumbling granite. In the south it is clay and limestone, covered with smooth pebbles. These round stones accumulated on the river bed at the end of the last Ice Age, when the river was a raging torrent. In places they are so abundant as to completely cover the arable land, as in Châteauneuf-du-Pape. These pebbles are an excellent temperature regulator, protecting the ground and absorbing heat during the day which they then transfer to the ground at night.

In the north the climate is fairly mild, hot in summer and somewhat cold in winter. The south has a Mediterranean climate with hot summers, mild winters and infrequent, heavy rainfall. Throughout the area there is the cool, strong northerly wind which has a considerable effect upon the growing conditions – the mistral.

Several grape varieties are grown in this area: in the north there is the red Syrah and the white Viognier, Marsanne and Roussanne. In the south there are about 20 different types, among them Grenache, Syrah, Mouvedre, Cinsault and Carigan (all reds) and Roussanne, Marsanne, Clairette and Ugni (all whites).

THE *CRUS*

Appellations d'origine contrôlées

Most of the wine produced in the Rhône valley comes from the southern half of the region.

Côtes du Rhône

Reds, whites and rosés. Reds are by far the most common, whites accounting for less than 1 per cent of the production. Under this generic *appellation* come some very diverse wines, their quality depending on the soil where the grapes were grown. The very great majority come from the Drôme or Vaucluse regions, or from the easterly parts of Gard.

These are generally robust, full bodied, generous, well rounded wines, reminiscent of the wines of Burgundy but without their distinction or vigour. A certain peppery quality is often a distinguishing feature of the reds.

The *appellation* Côtes du Rhône may be followed by the name of the department that the wine is from, for example, Rhône, Loire, Ardèche, Drôme, Vaucluse, Gard.

Côtes-du-Rhône-Villages

This is the name given to a wine which comes from one or more of the villages listed below. The high proportion of Grenache grapes in these wines makes them fuller and richer than the pure Côtes-du-Rhône. These villages may add their name to the general *appellation*:

- *Drome*: Rochegude, Saint-Maurice-sur–Aygues, Vinsobres, Rousset, Saint-Pantaléon.
- *Vaucluse*: Cairanne, Gigondas, Le Rasteau, Roaix, Séguret, Vacqueyras (may include Sarrians), Valréas, Visan.
- *Gard*: Laudun, renowned for its whites (may include Saint-Victor-Lacoste and Tresques); Chusclan, known for its reds and its excellent rosés (may include Orsan, Codolet, Bagnols-sur-Cèze, Saint-Étienne-des-Sorts, Cornillon, La Roque-sur-Cèze).

Condrieu

The northernmost vineyard, a mere 10 km from Vienne but on the right bank, produces an excellent dry white from the Viognier. Full of bouquet, light, elegant, powerful, full of flavour, and having a particularly original character.

Côte-Rôtie

Small neighbouring vineyard where the Syrah grape, blended with a small proportion of Viognier, produces a generous, powerful red wine with the distinctive taste that this grape gives. Laying down this wine produces an intense bouquet.

Château-Grillet

This vineyard, situated in Verin (Loire), has the distinction of being the smallest in France with its own *appellation contrôlée*. It produces a powerful white wine from the Viognier grape, sharply perfumed, with a distinctive quality about it. Unfortunately it is very difficult to find this wine.

Cornas
A robust, full bodied red wine made from Syrah grapes only, with a bouquet similar to that of Côte-Rôtie.

Saint-Peray
Produces a white wine with a clean taste and bouquet. It is especially known for its sparkling wine which is made by the champagne method.

Saint-Joseph
Produces mostly rich, powerful, aromatic reds from the Syrah grape only. There are also whites from the Marsanne and Roussanne grapes.

Crozes-Hermitage
Ten communes in Drôme, surrounding Hermitage, make this big, full bodied, smooth red wine made from the Syrah grape. There is also a dry, aromatic white, made in much smaller quantities (about one-tenth of production).

Hermitage
This *cru*, from the granite hill above the town of Tain, is of exceptional quality. The reds possess a fullness, a roundness, and a body comparable to the great wines of Burgundy. Laid down for long enough, their bouquet can be startling. The best vineyards are Le Bessards and Le Méal.

Only half as much white as red is produced, but it is equally respectable. It is a very powerful dry wine, and has an extremely fresh and original bouquet. The best *cru* is Chante-Alouette.

Clairette de Die
Produced from the Muscat grape over the whole Diois region high on the sides of the Drôme valley, this excellent sparkling wine could well be called the Asti of France.

Châtillon-en-Diois
These are reds, whites and rosés that are produced in a section of the Côte de Die designated area. Light and lively wines.

Coteaux du Tricastin
This is a vineyard comprising 20 or so communes on the border of the departments Drôme and Vaucluse (Saint-Paul-Trois-Chateaux). The reds are full bodied and hearty with a pleasant nose and are delightful when young. The rosés are excellent; they are clean and fruity, and have a delicate charm.

Châteauneuf-du-Pape
Ninety-six per cent of production is red. This is the best known *cru* of the southern Côtes-du-Rhône, partly because of the nostalgia it evokes, and partly because of its exceptional qualities that come from the principal grape variety, the Grenache. It is powerful, generous, big, fat and full bodied; keeps well and develops a sumptuous bouquet. Le Château de Fines-Roches is worth a special mention.

A rare dry white (1 per cent of total production) is remarkable for its calibre, its warmth and its finesse.

Rasteau
As well as some highly regarded red wines, this village, along with Cairanne and Sablet, produces a dessert wine that is full and fragrant and which, when aged a little, may be called 'rancio' (rancid).

Gigondas
This commune produces the best red and rosé wines of Upper Vaucluse; they are rich, full and fleshy.

Muscat de Beaumes-de-Venise
A dessert wine with a very distinctive nose.

Côtes-du-Ventoux
This is a huge area comprising 50 or so communes in the Apt region (Vaucluse), producing bright, fruity red and rosé wines that are lighter bodied than the Côtes du Rhône. Whites are rare.

Tavel
The best *cru* of the department and of the right bank Côtes du Rhône. It is a very full bodied rosé, extremely warm and heady, but sometimes a little too heavy.

Lirac
Produces some fairly full bodied reds, Tavel-type rosés and a little white.

Vins delimités de qualité supérieure

Côtes du Luberon
This is a charming region that is bordered by the Durance to the north and includes villages with names that ring like a Mistral poem; Merindol, Lourmarin, La Tour-d'Aigues, Pertuis, Cadenet, and so forth – 30 altogether, making wines that are light and refined, but free and easy and a little cheeky; reds, rosés and dry whites. The latter are valued for their fruitiness, finesse and liveliness.

Haut Comtat
Reds and rosés that are fairly solid and strong, from the Nyons area in Drôme.

Côtes du Vivarais
Principally reds and rosés from the southerly part of Ardèche and from a small area of land in Gard. These are solid wines, a little rough and tough, and bright red in colour. A few whites are found; they have a strong nose but age rapidly. The following are worth mentioning: Orgnac, Saint-Montant and Saint-Remèze.

Vins de pays

Vin de pays des coteaux de l'Ardèche is produced in the south and southeast of the department.

Vin de pays des coteaux des Baronnies (Drôme) comes from the southeast of the department (Buis-les-Baronnes, Nyons, etc).

Vin de pays de Principauté D'Orange (Vaucluse).

Vins de consommation courante

These are spread throughout all the departments that border onto the Rhône. The best are in Vaucluse and in the area of Gard that is next to the river. However, the tiny part of the department of Isère around Vienne deserves a special mention; reds from Seyssuel, whites from la Côte Saint-André, the Valentinois region and the Coulon valley to the north of Luberon.

14

PROVENCE
LANGUEDOC
CORSICA

Despite the fact that this is the most excellent winegrowing country, neither the Midi nor Corsica has any vineyards of great prestige, except those producing *vin doux naturels*, natural sweet wines.

In many districts winegrowing is the sole economic activity: the risks and traumas are great, but so too is the prosperity that can be won. The vine seems designed to thrive on these mostly poor soils. Its relatively easy and sometimes profitable cultivation pays the wages of more men per unit area than any other agricultural enterprise. At the same time, when crisis strikes the vine, it has an immediate and catastrophic effect on a huge number of people.

GROWING CONDITIONS

The southern vineyard is on two main types of land. On the one hand there are the hills of varying height, which rise between the mountains (the Alps, the Cévennes and the Pyrenees) and the sea, and on the other hand there are the plains that border the coastal rivers. On the hills, the vines grow on limestone scrubland or on granite hills as in Var, or on schist as in certain parts of Corbières. On the fertile plains of the valleys of the Vistre, the Vidourle, the Hérault, the Orb, the Aude, the Agly and the Tet, the vine has taken too strong a hold. The sands of the land along the coast and of Camargue complete the vineyard of Languedoc. In Corsica, the plain runs along the eastern coast, while the rest of the island has hillside vineyards.

The climate is typically Mediterranean with its mild winters, hot dry summers, infrequent but violent rains, and above all its winds, which may be fresh or violent, and influence the production greatly: the mild and humid Mistral, or the Marin.

Many different vines are grown; among the reds, the Carignan predominates, accounting for an increasing part of production year by year at the expense of its partners, but improving the general quality of the wines. The wine is a little rough but robust and powerful. The Aramon grape when planted on the plain produces a wine which is feeble, light and not very high in alcohol. If it is planted on a hill, however, it produces a light but delicate wine that is fruity and quite pleasant. The Aramon is extraordinarily successful in

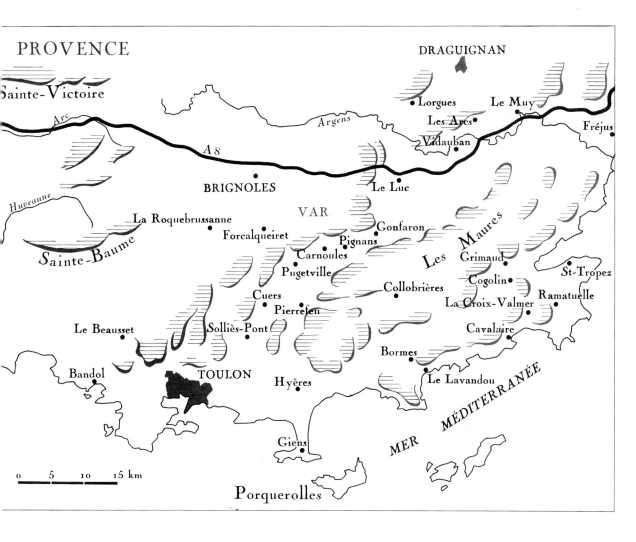

rich soils, and it is this characteristic which has allowed it gradually to progress down towards the lowlands, providing the winegrower with a quick profit. This development is to the detriment of the region as a whole, since it is mainly responsible for the overproduction of flat, anaemic wines. It is very difficult to sell these wines in years of plenty, and the industry can only use them by blending them with more robust wines to give them some substance; Algerian wines were once used in this way, but nowadays Italian wines have to be imported. This further aggravates the crisis caused by overproduction.

Other red vines grown here are Cinsault, Terret Bourret, Grenache, Alicante Bouschet and several rare local types, such as Mourvedre, Morrastel, Aspiran, Picpoule Noir and Syrah. The main white vines are Clairette and Ugni.

Vins doux naturels can only come from Grenache, Muscat, Malvoisie and Macabeo grapes.

THE *CRUS* OF PROVENCE

Appellations d'origine contrôlées

The Côtes-de-Provence produce by far the most significant wines in the region. The rosés are particularly pleasant, and are delightful and fruity when young. The reds are fewer in number and are quite full bodied and refined; they often have a pleasant flavour of the soil. The whites are dry and have solid depth and a seductive aroma, but they do not age well. Their production is only 5 per cent of that of the reds and rosés. There are one or two communes in this vast *appellation* area which do set themselves apart as producing better quality wines. The area extends to the best holdings in Var and Bouches-du-Rhône. Worth mentioning are Pierrefeu, Collobrières, Puget-Ville, Cuers and Carnoules in the south of the department of Var.

Cassis (BOUCHES-DU-RHÔNE)
Produces good quality dry red, white and rosé wines that are smooth and delicate. There are more whites than the others, and these are also the best known.

Bandol (VAR)
Offers an excellent rosé wine that needs to age for a few months before reaching its potential fullness. The whites are much less common (about 6 per cent of total production) but are worthy of interest. The reds, largely made from the Mourvedre grape, are rich and round, but need a while to develop.

Bellet (ALPES-MARITIMES)
Has only a limited production that is practically all reserved for the Nice area. The reds, whites and rosés are all light and refined and have a great deal of charm.

Palette (BOUCHES-DU-RHÔNE)
Mainly red wine made in the area around Aix-en-Provence. It is only harvested in very small quantities. It is a rich and very substantial wine that develops an attractive bouquet. Worth mentioning: Château Simone.

Coteaux d'Aix-en-Provence (A.O.C. FROM 1984)
Red, white and rosé wines of varying quality but usually quite drinkable, produced over a large area of Bouches-du-Rhône.

Coteaux des Baux (A.O.C. FROM 1984)
Produced in a few communes to the west of the Alpilles. The exceptional location of this small region results in some quite delicate, fruity and high quality wines.

Vins delimités de qualité supérieure

Coteaux de Pierrevert are the best red and rosé wines from the department of Basses-Alpes. There are practically no whites.

Vins de pays

Vin de pays des coteaux varois is pleasant, light bodied red and rosé wine produced in the Brignoles region of the department of Var.

Vin de pays des Maures comes from the vineyards near the Côte Varois.

Vin de pays de Petite Crau comes from the Châteaurenard region of Bouches-du-Rhône.

Vin de pays du Mont de Caume comes from the Toulon area.

Vin de pays d'Oc: the whole of Provence (the departments of Var, Vaucluse and Bouches-du-Rhône) has the right to use this vast *appellation*.

Vins de consommation courante

There are very many of these in Provence. The ones from the department of Var are in general better than those from Languedoc. Those from Bouches-du-Rhône are the more ordinary.

Vins de consommation courante account for 80 per cent of production in Bouches-du-Rhône and approximately 50 per cent in Var and Vaucluse.

THE *CRUS* OF LANGUEDOC

The viticultural area of Languedoc comprises the four departments of Hérault, Gard, Aude and Pyrénées-Orientales. They produce 40–50 per cent of the French harvest, and of this 80–85 per cent are reds which make up the large majority of table wines drunk in France.

Appellations d'origine contrôlées

Amongst the huge mass of Languedoc wines, there is one category of exceptionally high class: the *vins doux naturels*. These are produced from specific grape types, mainly Muscat, and are made by adding alcohol to the fermenting must. Fermentation stops as soon as the alcohol level is about 17°. The operation is conducted in such a way as to leave a certain amount of sugar in the wine which gives it its characteristic sweetness. These are very generous and powerful wines that are also extremely fragrant and have a creaminess and delicacy that have won them worldwide renown. They make excellent dessert wines.

Grand-Roussillon

This is produced mainly in the department of Pyrénées-Orientales. It may be called *rancio* (rancid) if it develops such a flavour (not a criticism).

Banyuls (PYRÉNÉES-ORIENTALES)

The *appellation Banyuls Grand Cru* is reserved for higher quality wines made from a more limited selection of grapes. There are Banyuls *rancio* and Banyuls *secs*, Banyuls *brut* or Banyuls *dry* which contain only a limited amount of sugar.

Maury (PYRÉNÉES-ORIENTALES)

Rivesaltes (MOSTLY PYRÉNÉES-ORIENTALES)
It may also be called *rancio*.

Muscat de Rivesaltes
Produced from the muscat grape only.

Muscat de Lunel (HÉRAULT)

Muscat de Frontignan or Frontignan (HÉRAULT)

Muscat de Mireval (HÉRAULT)

Muscat de Saint-Jean-de-Minervois (HÉRAULT)

Blanquette de Limoux (Vin de Blanquette)
An excellent sparkling wine, that is elegant and fragrant, produced in the department of Aude from a particular grape, the Mauzac (Blanquette), and by a second fermentation in the bottle, the champagne method. Although this effervescent wine does not have as much prestige as Champagne, it is highly respected in an unfortunately very small area in the Midi.

Limoux nature
The still wine from the same region as the above wine.

Minervois (A.O.C. FROM 1985)
This vineyard, in the south of Hérault and in the north of Aude produces mostly good quality red wines that are well balanced and have a clean taste. *Vin Noble de Minervois* is the name given to a slightly stronger wine.

Coteaux du Languedoc (A.O.C. FROM 1985)
These are delightful wines that are typical of Languedoc and almost exclusively reds. They are produced in the departments of Hérault and Aude, the vineyard running parallel to the southern Cévennes and reaching down to the sea in places. The following villages or groups of villages particularly stand out:

- Saint-Georges d'Orques: a red wine similar to a Montpellier. Its youthful aroma is extremely pleasing and is much enjoyed by the local consumers.
- Saint-Drézéry (Hérault): red.
- Quatorze (Aude): the vineyard is near Narbonne, producing mainly full and opulent red wines.
- La Clape (Aude): the tall limestone hills that rise between Narbonne and the sea produce rich, full bodied and smooth wines; reds, whites and rosés.
- Saint-Chinian (Hérault): one of the most beautiful locations and some of the best land in Hérault. About 20 communes produce a bright coloured, full red wine with a pronounced style. (A.O.C. from 1982.)
- Saint-Christol (Hérault): reds and rosés.
- Coteaux de Verargues (Hérault): reds and rosés.
- Picpoul-de-Pinet (Hérault): a white wine made mainly from the Picpoul grape. It is a powerful wine that has good flavour but tends to maderise (turn brown) quickly.

- Saint-Saturnin and Montpeyroux (Hérault): reds and rosés.
- Pic-Saint-Loup (Hérault): these are red, white and rosé wines that come from north of Montpellier and are quite light, delicate and fruity. The old people of the area still remember the Gravette de Corconne, an elegant and delicate rosé.
- Cabrières (Hérault): a very good rosé that is full, aromatic and generous.
- Faugères (Hérault): mostly red wines that have a very powerful body, and are solid and vigorous. (A.O.C. from 1982)
- Coteaux de la Méjanelle (Hérault): reds, whites and rosés from south of Montpellier.
- Cabardes or Côtes du Cabardes et de l'Orbiel: red and rosé wines from the northern part of Aude; they are very hard, tannic and a little untamed.
- Côtes de la Malpère (Aude): red and rosé wines that are light bodied but that have a delicate aroma when young.

Fitou (AUDE)

A very good red wine that comes from the best district of Corbières. The wine is powerful, muscular and sometimes a little harsh.

Clairette du Languedoc

This is a dry white wine made from the grape of the same name in the region of Paulhan (Hérault). It is extremely fragrant but ages rapidly. The *appellation* may also be used for a sweet dessert wine that is made here by the same method as the *vins doux naturels*. If a rancid flavour appears with age, it may be called *rancio*.

Clairette de Bellegarde

This is a very aromatic dry white wine from Costières du Gard.

Collioure (PYRÉNÉES-ORIENTALES)

This name refers to the red wines harvested in the Banyuls region. The production is very limited but the wine is nevertheless full and well rounded and ages well, developing an excellent bouquet.

Côtes-du-Roussillon (PYRÉNÉES-ORIENTALES)

This is the typical red wine of the eastern Pyrenees, its large production coming from two huge areas in the department, the Agly and Tet valleys in the north and Aspres in the south. The area around Fenouillèdes is well known for its robust and excellently balanced wines.

Côtes-du-Roussillon-Villages

These are the best wines selected from the above vineyard.

Latour de France and Caramany

These two best villages may add their names to the *appellation* Côtes-du-Roussillon.

There is also a local *eau-de-vie* with an *appellation contrôlée: Eau-de-vie de Faugères*.

Vins delimités de qualité supérieure

These are the good red wines of the Midi, in the finest Languedoc tradition.

Corbières (AUDE)

These are principally reds – full bodied and warm, they age well. They are produced on the high cliffs by the sea, between the River Aude and the border of the department of Pyrénées-Orientales. The best are called *Corbières Supérieurs*.

Costières du Gard

This attractive vineyard situated on the slopes that overlook the Camargue to the southeast of Nîmes produces white, red and rosé wines that are quite refined, light and have a pleasant flavour of the land.

Carcassonne: The harvest
(Photograph by J. P. Verney – Ministry of Agriculture archives)

Vins de pays

There are very many *vins de pays*, and these are the table wines that are drunk in the south. They are the wines that accompany everyday meals; they do not bring us the enchanting pleasures of some great orchestral piece; instead daily they hum for us the soft airs of a popular refrain, but are they any less worthy because of it?

Vins de pays d'Oc

These include all the good table wines from the departments of Ardèche, Aude, Bouches-du-Rhône, Gard, Hérault, Pyrénées-Orientales, Var and Vaucluse.

Their quality varies with the area of production, the grape types, the methods of winemaking and of keeping the wine, the vintage, and so on. Particularly good *vins de pays* are listed below:

Pyrénées-Orientales
  Coteaux des Fenouillèdes
  Vin de pays Catalan and vin de pays des Côtes Catalanes
  Les Vals d'Agly

Aude
  Hautrive en pays d'Aude
  Haute Vallée de l'Aude
  Val de Torgan
  Val d'Orbieu
  Cucugnan
  Vallée du Paradis
  Coteaux de la Cité de Carcassonne
  Coteaux du Termenès
  Val de Dagne
  Coteaux de la Cabrerisse
  Côtes de Pérignan
  Coteaux de Peyriac
  Val de Cesse
  Coteaux de Miramont
  Coteaux Cathares and Citadelles Cathares
  Coteaux du Lezignanais

Hérault
  Vins des Sables du Golfe du Lions
  Collines de la Moure
  Côtes de Thau
  Coteaux du Libron
  Coteaux de Laurens
  Coteaux de Murviel
  Coteaux du Salagou
  Côtes du Brian
  Vin de pays des gorges de l'Hérault
  Val de Montferrand
  Bessan

Caux
Cessenon
Côtes de Thongue
Haute Vallée de l'Orb
Vicomte d'Aumelas
Mont-Baudile
Côtes de Ceresson
Coteaux d'Enserune

Gard
Coteaux Flaviens
Coteaux du Salaves
Coteaux du Pont du Gard
Cerre de Coiran
Coteaux du Vidourle
Vins de pays de l'Uzège
Coteaux Cévenols
Mont-Bouquet
Vin de pays de la Vistrenque
Coteaux de Cèze
Vin de pays des Sables du Golfe du Lion
Vin de pays de Vaunage

Bouches du Rhone
Vin de pays des Sables du Golfe du Lion

In 1977 this list accounted for one quarter of the production of red table wines in the four departments and only 10 per cent of the whites. There may well be others to be added now.

Vins de consommation courante

These are all the other wines, the obscure wines, the ones that didn't make the grade, and the wines that are blended; they come from vineyards which may not be ideally situated; the wines may be better or worse according to the year. These are the 'infantry'; they have their merits and their weaknesses, and they have great difficulty surviving. The wines account for more than 60 per cent of the Languedoc production.

THE *CRUS* OF CORSICA

The old town of Cyrnos once witnessed much winemaking activity. During the centuries this has diminished to the cultivation of just a few indigenous vines for local consumption. The maquis vine was brought over by Algerian repatriates and planted here, causing a strong upsurge in wine production – nowadays this can reach two million hectolitres. On the island there are some high calibre red and rosé wines that are powerful, smooth and have a pronounced taste of the soil. The whites account for only 2 per cent of the total harvest.

The eastern plain is the area that produces table wines; the best *crus* come from the hills, and from the foothills of the mountains.

As well as the Languedoc vines, there are a few local ones which give the wines their character: Sciacarello Noir, Niellucio Noir; Vermentino Blanc.

Appellations d'origine contrôlées

Vin de Corse

Red, rosé or white. This is a full wine, having a certain amount of 'fire' due to its alcoholic strength, a good solid depth, a certain fatness; it can be smooth if the wine has been well made. The reds age quite well; the whites maderize quickly. Some vineyards enjoy their own *appellation*:

Patrimonio (at the lower eastern edge of the headland)
Coteaux d'Ajaccio or Ajaccio
Sartene

Calvi
Coteaux du Cap Corse
Figari
Porto Vecchio.

The production accounts for 10 per cent of the island's wines.

There is no *vin delimité de qualité supérieure* from Corsica.

Vins de pays

One single category includes all the better table wines: *Vins de pays de l'Ile-de-Beauté*. These are lighter, less well rounded wines, but they are smooth and have a characteristic aroma.

Vins de consommation courante

This is the source of the great majority of high calibre French wines used in commercial blending. Their body is an effective corrective to the thinness of some mainland wines. Certain large cooperatives such as Aleria and Ghisonaccia produce significant quantities of them.

One or two dessert wines of the Malaga or Madeira type come from the Cap Corse.

15

CENTRAL PLATEAU
BOURBONNAIS
BERRY-NIVERNAIS

Auvergne and Bourbonnais, or at least the five departments that come under these names (Puy-de-Dôme, Allier, Loire, Cantal, Haute-Loire), do not play a significant rôle in French viticulture, since the total area reserved for wine production represents only 1 per cent of France's vineyards. The Berry region extends from Auvergne and Bourbonnais towards the Loire. This is also not generally a winegrowing part of the country, although there are some small areas that continue to produce some very likeable wines. The viticultural activity in Nivernais is confined to the Pouilly region which is separated from Sancerre by the Loire; the two vineyards face each other from opposite banks of the river.

GROWING CONDITIONS

The soils in this vast area vary tremendously, from the primary granite or schist landscapes of the Auvergne mountains to the clay or sandy soils of the valleys, or the limestone soils of Pouilly and Sancerre.

Most of the vineyards are situated on the hills that form the slopes of the river valleys of the Loire, the Cher, the Arnon and the Sioule. The climate is generally quite continental and spring frosts are always a possibility.

The vines are a combination of Burgundy types – Pinot, Chardonnay and, especially, Gamay – and vines from the Loire valley, such as the Sauvignon, along with a few local ones, such as the white Tressalier from Saint-Pourçain.

THE *CRUS*

Appellations d'origine contrôlées

Sancerre (CHER)
Sancerre and a few neighbouring communes have a very dense vineyard that produces some well respected white wines from the Sauvignon grape. These are dry, extremely fragrant, and delicate wines, quite smooth and elegant, and with a clean, crisp aroma if grown on limey soils, less refined if on clay soils. They do not age well.

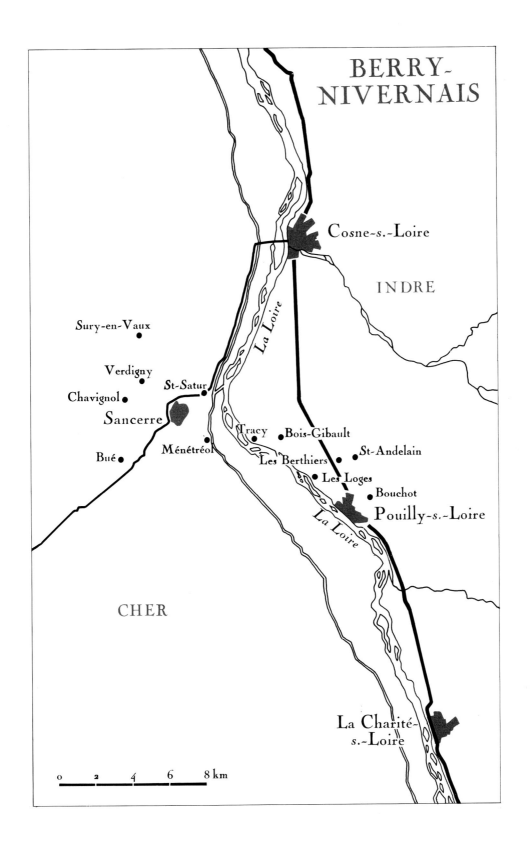

BERRY-
NIVERNAIS

Cosne-s.-Loire

INDRE

Sury-en-Vaux

La Loire

Verdigny

St-Satur

Chavignol

Sancerre

Tracy

Bois-Gibault

St-Andelain

Ménétréol

Les Berthiers

Bué

Les Loges

Bouchot

Pouilly-s.-Loire

La Loire

CHER

La Charité-
s.-Loire

0   2   4   6   8 km

Pinot Noir

Cabernet Sauvignon

Grenache

Riesling

Chardonnay

(Photographs by Pierre Mackiewicz – Institut Technique du Vin)

The hamlets of Chavignol. Saint-Satur, Bué (Clos de la Poussie) are particularly good.

The Pinot Noir makes very pleasant fruity rosés and a few round, fairly full bodied reds that develop a good bouquet after a while. Together, they only account for 20 per cent of the total harvest.

Pouilly fumé or Blanc fumé de Pouilly (NIÈVRE)

Fumé is the name given to the Sauvignon grape on this bank of the Loire. No sweet wines are made in this tiny vineyard, and the dry white is fairly similar to the wine from Sancerre, just across the river; however, it does tend to be fuller, and often more delicate; it also ages better even though it is still an aromatic 'new wine'.

The hamlets of les Loges, Bouchet and Bois Gibault (in the commune of Tracy) particularly stand out, as does the commune of Saint-Andelain.

Pouilly-sur-Loire

On the same land, the Chasselas vine is also cultivated. It may or may not be blended with Sauvignon, but in either case benefits from this *appellation*. It is a dry white wine that is a little less round but quite solid, has a less intense aroma and more pronounced acidity.

Quincy (CHER)

This small vineyard produces lively dry white wines that are somewhat acidic but have the so-called 'gun-flint' flavour that is so characteristic of a Sauvignon.

Reuilly

On the border between the departments of Indre and Cher, Reuilly offers some eminently drinkable Sauvignon whites of the Quincy type; also fruity rosés and light, delicate reds from Pinot grapes. The amounts harvested are very limited.

Menetou-Salon (CHER)

These Sauvignon whites, and Pinot rosés and reds, each have a pleasant character in their own way, and are all attractive.

Vins delimités de qualité supérieure

Saint-Pourçain-Sur-Sioule (ALLIER)

This very old vineyard enjoys a very good local reputation. Its fame is beginning to spread because of the excellent wines it can offer. Unfortunately, in some years the weather conditions can cause a great deal of damage and the quality varies greatly from one vintage to another.

The whites are produced mostly from the Tressalier grape and have great finesse, are very elegant, and at their best may even be reminiscent of the *vins de nature* of Champagne (the white wine that is produced in the Champagne region and is not made into Champagne). They account for approximately a quarter of production.

The reds and rosés, from the Gamay and Pinot grapes are more similar to the Burgundy Passe-Tout-Grain.

Côtes d'Auvergne (PUY-DE-DÔME)

The Clermont-Ferrand district produces Gamay and Pinot red wines that at their best come close to a Beaujolais red. Worth looking out for are Chanturgue, Chateaugay, Boudes and Madargues. The rosés are delightful when young. There are hardly any Chardonnay whites.

Côtes du Forez (LOIRE)

Reds and rosés only, made from Gamay grapes; these wines are pleasant when young. The entire production is consumed locally.

Côtes Roannaises (LOIRE)

Produces Gamay reds and rosés that are not dissimilar to the Côtes du Forez wines.

Valencay (INDRE)

Mostly reds and rosés that are quite strong and vigorous and can take a certain amount of ageing; they are produced from a combination of Bordeaux and Val de Loire grape types. The whites (20 per cent) are more varied but can be very pleasing and fruity despite their lightness. It is very rare to find this wine.

Châteaumeillant

On the border of Indre and Cher, this vineyard produces pale coloured, light bodied reds and rosés that have a pleasant aroma in a good year. Again, very rarely found.

Vins de pays

Vin de pays du Jardin de la France (Cher and Indre).
  Vin de pays de Cher

Vins de consommation courante

The table wines produced in this vast region are low quality wines that are often thin and empty. They are almost all reds.

16

THE LOIRE VALLEY

This is the 'Garden of France'. Grapes of many different varieties grow here in abundance. From Orléans to Nantes, by way of Touraine and Anjou, flourishing vineyards and royal *châteaux* make this a spectacular part of the country.

GROWING CONDITIONS

On the hillsides around the Loire and its tributaries the vineyards produce numerous high quality *crus*.

The soil is clay or sandy in the lower-lying parts but the essential characteristic of this area is the tufa rock – the chalk that is found all along the river banks, both in Touraine and in the eastern part of Anjou. In the picturesque landscape of Anjou and Touraine, there are splendid limestone blocks where caves have been hollowed out. Covering the chalk is a layer of clayey limestone that varies in thickness; this layer makes it possible for the vine to fix its roots. To the west of Anjou the soil is similar to that of Brittany: schist and granite. In Loire-Atlantique vines grow on hard or fractured rocks.

The climate is mild and wet with the danger of spring frosts. This is the most northerly winegrowing region, and good sunny years are needed to give these wines that are the glory of Anjou and Touraine all their warmth and brilliance.

The vines used to produce red wines are from Bordeaux: Cabernet Franc (locally known as Breton), Cabernet-Sauvignon, Cot (or Malbec), together with Gamay, Groslot, and Meunier (an indigenous vine which has a pale grape). Pinot d'Aunis and some Pinot Noirs and Pinot Gris (sometimes called Malvoisie) are also used.

The principal grape used to make the better white wines is the Chenin (or Pinot de la Loire). There are also some Meslier (or Menu Pinot), Sauvignon and Chardonnay vines.

In Loire-Atlantique, only one vine deserves to be mentioned: Muscadet.

In Poitou, both Loire and Bordeaux vines are cultivated in several areas.

THE *CRUS*

Appellations d'origine contrôlées

The *appellation d'origine contrôlée* wines of Touraine and Anjou as well as those of Loire-Atlantique, Berry and Nivernais may be followed by the words *Val de Loire*.

Touraine

This *appellation* is the generic A.O.C. for the large number of red, rosé and dry white wines from the departments of Indre-et-Loire and Loir-et-Cher. Their quality varies tremendously, although in general they are light, lively and fruity wines but have pronounced acidity in a bad year.

Touraine mousseux

Obtained by secondary fermentation in the bottle, as are all the sparkling wines of the Loire. There are certain similarities here with Champagne: the extremely chalky soil, the mild climate, the cellars carved out of the rock so as to maintain an even temperature, the production of sparkling wines by the champagne method itself. All this produces some very fine wine with an original and distinctive taste, a good bouquet and delicate sparkle. However, it does not have the sheer breeding or elegance of a Marne wine.

Crémant de la Loire

The sparkling wine that is produced over the whole of Touraine, Anjou and Saumur.

Touraine pétillant

The particularly attractive quality of this wine is its soft, gentle bubbliness that puts it somewhere between still and sparkling wines.

Touraine-Ambroise (INDRE-ET-LOIRE)

Its production is confined to eight communes surrounding Ambroise.

Touraine-Mesland

Touraine-Azay-le-Rideau

Vouvray (INDRE-ET-LOIRE)

This charming village on the east bank of the Loire, along with its seven neighbours, produces a Chenin white wine that is very fragrant, full, and dry, medium dry or, in good years, sweet. Its finesse and the strength that it develops with age combine to make this a top class wine. A particular advantage of this wine is that although it is very pleasing while still young it ages extremely well and acquires a distinctive flavour which can be likened to that of ripe quince. The Coquette and Chartier valleys have the best estates, and Clos Baudoin (Nouy Valley) is worth mentioning.

Vouvray mousseux and Vouvray pétillant

Château de Moncontour is a notable wine.

Montlouis (INDRE-ET-LOIRE)

Across from Vouvray on the south bank of the Loire this vineyard produces wines of a similar type that may be dry or sweet, but although they may be very

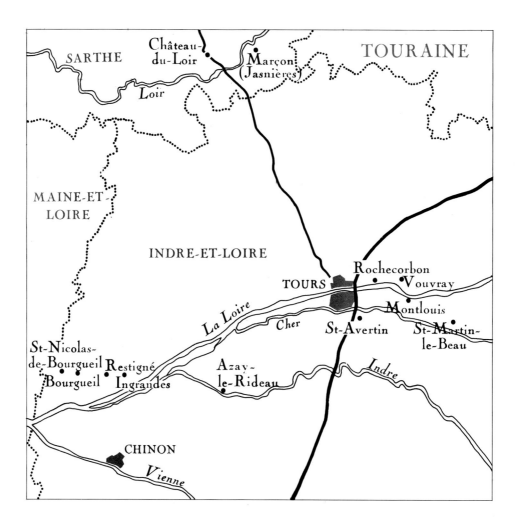

high class, less favourable growing conditions mean that they do not reach the same level of quality.

Montlouis mousseux and Montlouis pétillant

Bourgueil

This vineyard combines eight villages within the eastern limits of the Indre-et-Loire. Vines of Cabernet Franc and Cabernet-Sauvignon are densely planted, producing a red wine with a deep purplish colour that is quite harsh when young but is also robust, solid and powerful, and with age develops a remarkable bouquet and becomes a high-class wine with very attractive character.

This is the most northerly point at which the Cabernet vine is grown, and unfortunately its sensitivity to the lack of sunshine means, unfortunately, that quality varies greatly from year to year.

Saint-Nicholas-de-Bourgueil

The best village in the Bourgueil area, its wines being the most well balanced and most satisfying. They have a raspberry-like bouquet.

Chinon (INDRE-ET-LOIRE)

This important vineyard is spread around the confluence of the Vienne and the Loire. It is also planted with Cabernet vines and produces a red wine that is not dissimilar to a Bourgueil – just as delicate and as full and with as good a colour, but having a slightly different, violet-like quality about it. It keeps very well indeed and is, like a Bourgueil, a wine worth being patient with to allow its bouquet to hatch.

White Chenin wines are produced here, but only in very small quantities.

Les Coteaux du Loire

An area of about 20 communes on the border of the departments of Sarthe and Indre-et-Loire. Their production is very limited. The reds are light and fruity, the whites, which are both dry and sweet, are made from the Chenin grape and age well.

Jasnières (SARTHE)

Two small communes on the edge of the Loire are particularly well known for their production of a very dry white Chenin wine that is lively, has an extremely sharp flavour that may even be acidic, and also has a really delicate bouquet.

Anjou

The region that may use this *appellation* is vast; almost all of the department of Maine-et-Loire, a significant area of Deux-Sèvres and a small part of Vienne. The whites are generally sweet, have a good bouquet, and are satisfying and pleasantly rounded. Their finesse and breed varies according to the area of production. There are as many reds as whites, and these are medium bodied, round, and age well, developing a pleasant bouquet.

Rosé d'Anjou

This is by far Anjou's most important product. The wines range from dry to sweet, are smooth and often pale in colour. They have a very characteristic charm and are pleasantly distinguished.

Cabernet d'Anjou

This is a dry to medium dry rosé made exclusively from Cabernet Franc and Cabernet-Sauvignon grapes. It is more refined, more elegant, and higher class than the rosé de Groslot.

Rosé de Loire

Applies to the dry rosés from Touraine, Anjou, or Saumur.

Anjou mousseux and Anjou pétillant

The region produces quite a large quantity of these sparkling whites or rosés that are sometimes of very good quality. The champagne method is used.

Saumur (MAINE-ET-LOIRE)

In general the whites are dry, fruity, smooth and distinguished, but there are also some which are very faintly sweet; a small amount of sugar is added to

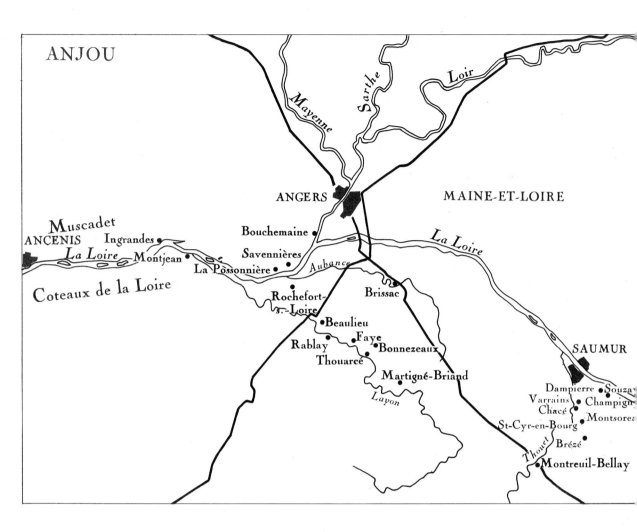

them which gives them their attractiveness. The reds are very similar to the Anjou reds, but are produced in much smaller quantities. The best is Saumur-Champigny. The rosés have the same style as the Rosés d'Anjou.

Saumur-Champigny

This is a full bodied and satisfying red wine made from the Cabernet grape; it should be kept to allow it to develop its excellent bouquet that is both powerful and delicate. Its large harvest comes from the villages along the Loire: Souzay, Chacé, Dampierre, Parnay, Saint-Cyr-en-Bourg, Saumur and Varrains.

Cabernet de Saumur

This sweetish rosé is far less common than its Anjou counterpart (12 to 15 per cent). It is often drier and less full.

Saumur mousseux and Saumur pétillant

These represent a selection of this style of wine from the vast Anjou region, made by the champagne method.

Anjou – Coteaux de la Loire

Mostly situated on the east bank of the river, and to the west of Angers, these vineyards produce the most delicate and elegant of the sweet Anjou wines. Their incomparable vigour and opulence rank them among the top sweet white wines of France, and they age admirably. Dry wines are sometimes made, but these are not nearly so successful.

Savennières

The best commune on the slopes of the Loire valley. These are very high class and extremely well respected dry white wines made from the Chenin grape. It is worth mentioning Château d'Epiré, la Coulée de Serrant, la Roche-aux-Moines, le Clos du Papillon.

Anjou – Coteaux de l'Aubance

Less striking but just as generous, these are the dry or sweet white wines that come from the hillsides along this small river that runs into the Loire from the west, just south of Angers.

Anjou – Coteaux du Layon

This name may or may not be followed by the name of the commune of origin. These sweet white wines from Layon are particularly full, powerful, and develop marvellously. They are a little less distinguished than the wines from the Loire hillsides, but are fatter, bigger and rounder. They age very well and can be kept for many years.

Coteaux du Layon-Chaume

The fullest and most generous of the above wines, they come from the commune of Rochefort-sur-Loire. Le Quarts-de-Chaume is worth mentioning since it has its own *appellation*. Le Château de Bellrive is a good estate.

Bonnezaux (COMMUNE OF THOUARCÉ)

Soft, velvety wines that have a long finish and a good bouquet. Le Château de Fesles is worth noting, and the villages of Rablay and Faye are also particularly good.

Anjou – Coteaux de Saumur

These are the sweet white wines from the region that is upstream of Saumur, in the direction of Montsoreau. They are not very abundant and are lighter, easier, more nervy and more virile than the Coteaux du Layon.

Muscadet

This is perhaps the most popular of all French white wines, the one that is drunk on romantic holidays in Brittany, and a very good accompaniment to seafood. Muscadet is the name of the grape, and not of the area as in most *appellations d'origine contrôlées*. The vine is a variety of the Burgundy Melon and produces a very dry wine with a discreet but characteristic aroma. It is vigorous, medium bodied and smooth, sometimes slightly green, and with a certain charm. It does, however, have the disadvantage of not ageing well.

The winegrowing areas are in Loire-Atlantique upstream from Nantes on both banks of the Loire.

Muscadet de Sèvre et Maine

This is most certainly the fruitiest, the most satisfying, and the best Muscadet. The vineyard is very dense and is situated on the western bank of the river, surrounding the best villages. These are Saint-Fiacre, La Haie-Fouassière, Vertou, La Chapelle-Heulin, Le Pallet, Vallet, and a few others.

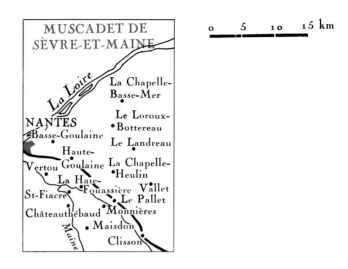

Muscadet des Coteaux de la Loire

This comes from a region that is less intensively viticultural and is near Ancenis on both sides of the estuary. The wine is pleasant enough but is less attractive and not as smooth as the Muscadet de Sèvre et Maine.

Muscadet-sur-Lie

These are the Muscadets that have been stored in vats or casks for the whole winter following the harvest without being racked; thus they are left on their lees. They are bottled in the spring, and have a more pronounced flavour and more intense aroma.

Vins delimités de qualité supérieure

Vins de l'Orléanais

Reds, rosés and whites that come from both banks of the Loire. They are light bodied and pale but fresh and fruity, and are made mostly from the Gris-Meunier and Meslier grapes.

Coteaux du Giennois (CÔTES DE GIEN)

White wines are made from Sauvignon and Chenin grapes, reds from Gamay and Pinot; there are also various rosés. Cosne-sur-Loire may be added to the *appellation*.

Coteaux du Vendomois

A large area of Loir-et-Cher adjacent to Beauce produces wines of varying quality that are fairly acidic and quite thin but in a good year can be lively; the whites are made from Chenin and Chardonnay grapes, the rosés mainly from Pinot d'Aunis to produce a pale, lively and nervy wine, and to complete the picture there are reds from Gamay, Pinot and Cabernet grapes. The rosés are the most important.

Cheverny

Cheverny is the centre of a vineyard of 20 or so communes producing wines that deserve some attention and respect. The Sauvignon whites are well known for the intensity of their aroma, their finesse and their distinctive character. Some very pleasant reds and rosés with a good nose are made from the Loire grapes, from Gamay to Cabernet, and their quality varies tremendously according to where they are made and the growing conditions, particularly the amount of rain during the year.

Coteaux d'Ancenis

White wines from Chenin and Pinot Gris (the grape variety must be stated after the name), reminiscent of a Saumur wine. The reds and rosés are from Cabernet and Gamay; they are light and have good fruit if the sun has been kind to them. The area of production extends from the border of Maine-et-Loire to the border of Loire-Atlantique.

Gros-Plant du Pays Nantais

This is the white wine of the Atlantic coast, and comes mostly from the district of Nantes. It is very dry, coarse, and lacks fruit, but is very lively and has an aggressive and tart flavour that attracts a lot of followers. Gros Plant is the local name for the Folle Blanche of Charentes.

Vins du Haut Poitou

Whites, reds and rosés of varying quality that are produced principally in the department of Vienne in the Neuville-de-Poitou region.

Vins du Thouarsais

White Chenin wines are light, carefree, and cheerful and very pleasant in a good year. Cabernet reds can also produce some reasonable bottles of wine.

Vins de pays

It is mostly the white wines that are of interest here, as long as they do justice to their Sauvignon origins. However, there are also quite a few red wines made from Gamay grapes which can have a certain gutsy style that is not without merit.

- *Vin de pays du département du Loir-et-Cher*
- *Vin de pays du département d'Indre-et-Loire*
- *Vin de pays du Jardin de France* (Loiret, Loir-et-Cher, Indre-et-Loire, Maine-et-Loire)
- *Vin de pays de Loire-Atlantique*
- *Vin de pays des Marches de Bretagne*: these last two originate from the Muscadet area, from part of Maine-et-Loire, and from Vendée.

- *Vin de pays de Retz*: south of the estuary and surrounding Grandlieu Lake.
- *Vin de pays des fiefs vendéens*: in the Mareuil, Brem, Vix, Pissotte and Valmondais regions.

Vins de consommation courante

These are very abundant in the whole of the Val du Loire area, especially in Loir-et-Cher and Indre-et-Loire. They account for 60 per cent of regional production and for 5 per cent of French *vins de consommation courante*.

Naturally light and usually not very strong in alcohol, they only have body if some sugar is added to the grapes, a process known as chaptalisation. They are therefore a good ingredient in commercial blendings to which they bring a lightness, a certain fruitiness and maybe some colour if they are produced from deep coloured grapes. Many of the white wines are drunk as they are since their acidity does not make them too harsh.

The *rougets de Poitou*, very light and pale red wines, also have their admirers.

17
CHAMPAGNE

Champagne is renowned throughout the world. People who know nothing else about France, know about Champagne, and it conjures up a sense of frivolity, celebration and sparkle. No ambassador can have earned his country more prestige than Champagne has earned for France.

Most of the Champagne vineyard is in the department of Marne, the remainder being in Aisne and Aube.

GROWING CONDITIONS

The soil is made up of compacted chalk on a layer of unstable soil; this layer is of varying depth and is of quite poor quality. The landscape is made up of low hills, often capped with small woods, and it is at the foot of these hills that the vines flourish.

The vineyards are planted with two principal vines, the red Pinot Noir and the white Chardonnay, as in Burgundy, except that here the black grape is used to make white wine. The Pinot accounts for a larger proportion of the vines, in fact it is often the only type grown; in the southern part of the region, however, on the 'Côte des Blancs', only Chardonnay is grown. The wine that is made from the white grape is lighter and more delicate and has a more striking bouquet; wine from the red grape has more body and fullness.

It is the skill of each individual winemaker in blending the two wines that counts in obtaining the best results.

The *appellation d'origine contrôlée Coteaux Champenoise* is given to the *vin nature*, as it is after fermentation. It may be red, white or rosé. The white accounts for 80 per cent of production and has exceptional lightness, delicacy and elegance. It acquires a remarkable bouquet that is attractively and distinctively sappy. These are the qualities that are shown off to their best advantage by the addition of a fine, sparkling foam or *mousse*.

The rosés and the reds are medium bodied but alcoholic, well balanced and develop lovely bouquets if kept for long enough. The Bouzy region is the most famous.

Champagne

The *appellation* is restricted to those wines that have undergone a secondary fermentation in the bottle, producing enough gas to make them effervescent. The method of doing this is attributed to Dom Perignon, a Benedictine monk and procurator of Hautvilliers Abbey from 1668 until his death in 1715. Dom Perignon is also said to have been the first to use cork to seal the bottles, something that is essential for preserving the sparkle.

The dry white wine is bottled in the spring following the harvest. Enough cane sugar is then added to create the desired pressure inside the bottle, along with an active yeast culture, a small amount of tannin and a fining substance. The cork is then held on by a wire clasp, or a metal cap.

Next, the bottles are piled up horizontally. The action of the yeast breaks down the sugar into alcohol, which increases the strength of the wine, and carbon dioxide; since this cannot escape it is absorbed into the wine, increasing the pressure inside the bottle to something in the order of six atmospheres.

When all the sugar has been converted, the yeast sinks, pulled down by the tannin and the fining, forming a kind of gel. A large amount of opaque deposit settles along the length of the horizontal bottle. This completes the *prise de mousse* (literally, 'capturing the froth') period. The bottles are stored in this position for a certain amount of time, sometimes one or two years.

For all these procedures a cool, stable temperature is essential, and the *crayères*, the extraordinary underground cellars carved in the surrounding chalk, provide the optimum conditions.

After being left to rest for a while the bottles are placed on *pupitres*, racks made from two rectangular boards hinged together in an inverted V position; the neck of the bottle is tilted downwards to allow the sediment to move gradually towards the cork. The bottle is turned about its axis one-eighth of a turn, while at the same time the angle of the tilt is increased. This operation is called *remuage* and can be carried out manually or by machine. The bottle undergoes this process every other day, and when it has completed three full turns it is in an almost vertical position and all the sediment is resting on the cork. The bottle is then kept upside down to await the process of *dégorgement*. This used to be done *à la volée*: the bottle was held upside down and the clasp removed; the pressure of the gas pushed the cork and the sediment violently out; the bottle was swiftly turned upright again and a rubber cork was inserted until the next operation, the *dosage*. Champagne producers nowadays prefer *dégorgement à la glace*: the neck of the bottle is immersed in a bath of freezing brine; the sediment turns to an icy mush, allowing for a swifter and more economical *dégorgement*, since the bottles can be upright. During this process the interior pressure of the bottle falls by about half.

The next stage – the *dosage* – is to fill up the partially emptied bottle from another bottle, at the same time adding a *liqueur d'expédition* (a wine of a similar but traditionally older *cuvée* that is sweetened) to give the wine a certain sweet smoothness. Various degrees of sweetness are obtained, depending on the amount added: *brut*, *extra-sec* (extra dry), *gout americain* (American taste), *demi-doux* (medium sweet), and *doux* (sweet). *Brut* is generally reserved for the best *cuvées*.

The bottle is then recorked and a wire clasp holds the new cork in place. All

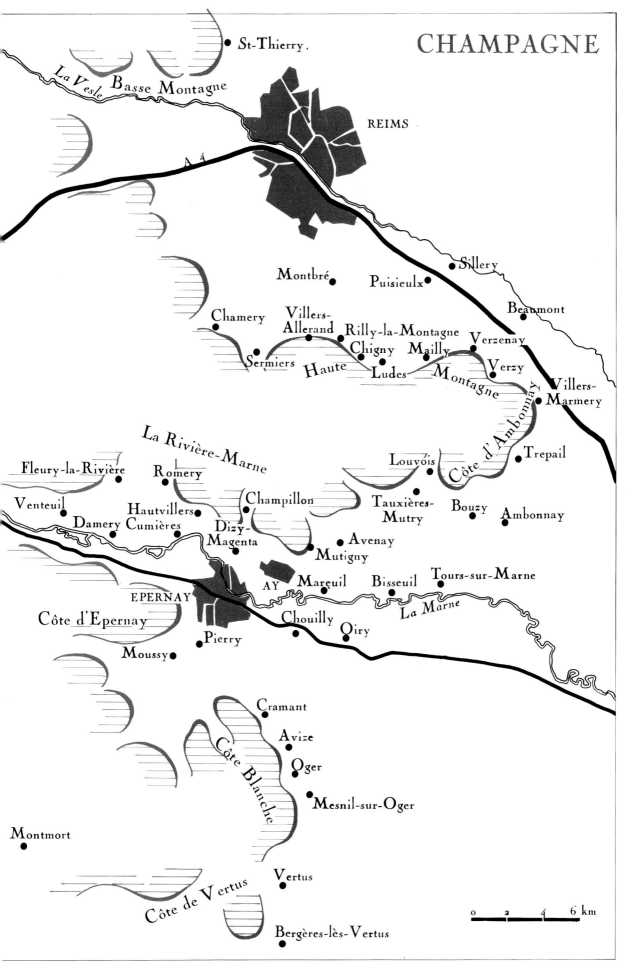

CHAMPAGNE

St-Thierry

La Vesle   Basse Montagne

REIMS

A 4

Sillery

Montbré   Puisieulx

Beaumont

Chamery   Villers-Allerand   Rilly-la-Montagne   Verzenay

Chigny   Mailly   Verzy

Sermiers   Haute   Ludes   Montagne   Villers-Marmery

Côte d'Ambonnay

La Rivière-Marne   Louvois   Trepail

Fleury-la-Rivière   Romery   Champillon   Tauxières-Mutry   Bouzy   Ambonnay

Venteuil

Hautvillers   Dizy-Magenta

Damery   Cumières   Avenay

Mutigny

AY   Mareuil   Bisseuil   Tours-sur-Marne

EPERNAY   La Marne

Côte d'Epernay   Chouilly   Oiry

Pierry

Moussy

Cramant

Avize

Oger

Côte Blanche   Mesnil-sur-Oger

Montmort

Vertus

Côte de Vertus

Bergères-lès-Vertus

0   2   4   6 km

Champagne: The harvest
(Photograph by J. P. Verney – Ministry of Agriculture archives)

that remains now is for the wine to age a little before being dressed for sale. Vintage Champagne must be at least three years old before being retailed, but it should be watched carefully since it will not last forever.

A *crémant* Champagne is one that is made with less carbonation, so is less effervescent. In this case, 'sparkling' means just a few bubbles rising from the side of the glass.

Champagne rosé – pink Champagne – is obtained by adding a good *cru* red wine to the *cuvée*.

The conditions under which Champagne is produced, harvested, made, aged and sold are rigorously defined by law and inspected by the Comité interprofessionel des vins de Champagne.

Champagne: Remuage
(Photograph by J. P. Verney – Ministry of Agriculture archives)

Champagne is offered to the consumer under the trade name of the producer, not the place of origin, as is usually the case with other wines. There are about 130 handlers and traders in Champagne, from owner-growers to merchants, from small producers to huge enterprises. But it is a fact that the same ones always produce the best results: experience and, above all, the art of the producer are everything when it comes to making Champagne.

The Champagne area is divided into different zones, and each zone is given a value coefficient; it is on this basis that the price of the grapes is decided.

● The Valley of the River Marne zone:
These are often the most esteemed, having a subtle flavour and a delicate bouquet.
    Ay, Mareuil, Dizy-Magenta, Avenay, Champillon, Mutigny, Cumières, Hautvillers and Bisseuil.
● The Côte d'Ambonnay or intermediate zone:
These are remarkable wines; robust, nervy, vigorous and well rounded; they are valued for their verve and solidity.
    Ambonnay, Bouzy, Louvois, Tours-sur-Marne and Tauxières-Mutry.

● The Côte d'Épernay:
On the left bank of the Marne, across from the Ay region, this zone produces slightly less distinguished wines; they are, however, full bodied and robust.

Chouilly, Pierry, Épernay and Moussy.

● The Côte d'Avize or Côte Blanche:
Chardonnay is the predominant grape here, producing the famous *Blancs de Blancs* that take longer to develop but are more delicate and have greater finesse. They are particularly known for their grace, their elegance, and their 'lacy' quality.

Avize, Cramant, Oger, Oiry and Mesnil-sur-Oger. The Monthelon, Grauves and Cuis vineyards are planted with both red and white vines.

● The Côte de Vertus:
This zone has the most solid wines.

Vertus and Bergères-les-Vertus.

● The Montagne de Reims zone:
This is subdivided into:

   ● Haute-Montagne: rich, full bodied wines that have a good freshness and develop an excellent bouquet.

    Sillery, Beaumont-sur-Vesles, Verzenay, Mailly, Verzy, Rilly-la-Montagne, Ludes, Chigny-les-Roses, Trépail, Villers-Marmery, Villers-Allerand, Puiseulx, Chamery, Montbré and Sermiers.

   ● Basse (Lower)-Montagne to the northwest of Reims, the Saint-Thierry region.

● The Vignoble de l'Ouest:
This is an extension of the two preceding zones. The canton of Ville-en-Tardenois is the most interesting here, still having some good *crus* such as those from *la petite montagne*.

Sacy, Ecueil and Villedommange in the east and Vallée de l'Ardre in the west.

● The department of Aube includes two main areas that are authorised to produce Champagne. These are Bar-sur-Seine and Bar-sur-Aube, about 70 communes in all.

● The 90 communes in the department of Aisne may also use the *appellation*.

● Two communes in Haute-Marne and five in Seine-et-Marne are at the limits of the designated Champagne area.

The average yearly production of wine made under this *appellation* is some 1,300,000 hectolitres.

Rosé de Riceys (AUBE)

Appellation d'origine contrôlée. This wine is produced from the Pinot Noir and is light, lively and fragrant. Its production is extremely limited.

18

LORRAINE ALSACE

The vine is present throughout the Vosges mountains, but whereas the vineyard of Lorraine is one of the smallest, the vineyard of Alsace is quite large and has a wide reputation.

GROWING CONDITIONS

Lorraine is generally limestone and the vines that are grown here are principally from Burgundy along with a few from Alsace. In Alsace, the vine flourishes between the forest that caps the mountains and the Rhine plain. The best *crus* are found at the bottom of the slopes.

The harsh continental climate forces the growers to choose vines that do not mind the cold, that is the ones that are found in all the Rhine areas and throughout central Europe. This plays a bigger part in establishing the character of the wine than does the place of origin.

THE *CRUS*

Appellations d'origine contrôlées

Vin d'Alsace or Alsace
This is the generic *appellation* for all the wines from Haut-Rhin or Bas-Rhin that comply with the conditions imposed by the decrees of classification. The name of the commune or *cru* of origin may be added to it, along with the grape type. Here is a list of several grape types, in order of importance (only grapes from select 'noble' vines may be used): Gewurztraminer, Riesling, Pinot Gris (or Tokay), Muscat, Pinot Blanc (or Klevner), Sylvaner for the whites, Pinot Noir for the reds.

In Alsace, only white wines are of any significance, reds and rosés representing only 3 per cent of total production. They are very dry and extremely aromatic wines that can be kept for several years without losing any of their character.

The Riesling is the most delicate, elegant and easy-going. Its pale colour, the very light *petillance* that it often has (a small amount of gas remains from the

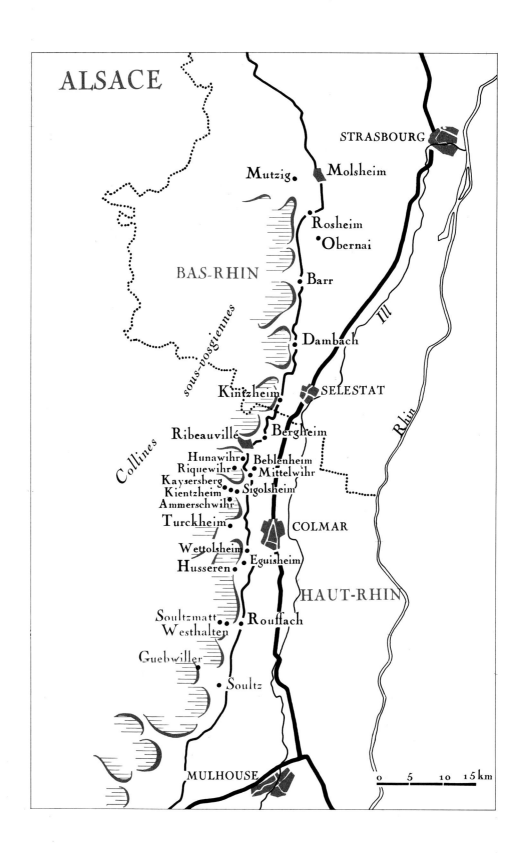

Alsace: Huawihr
(Photograph by Pierre Mackiewicz – Institut Technique du Vin)

fermentation), and its subtle fragrance all go to make it one of the top French wines; but a cold year will give it pronounced acidity which detracts from its attractiveness.

The pale pink skinned Gewurztraminer (and the Traminer which is not really in use now) has a much more accentuated fragrance, a very pronounced character, and a much bigger body. Both are therefore less elegant, but their power and originality mean that they are often preferred to the more discreet Riesling.

The Pinot Gris, or Tokay, as it is called here, has nothing in common with the famous sweet wine of Hungary which comes from another plant, the Furmint. The origins of this nickname have been variously interpreted, but it probably comes from the name that used to be given to dessert wines that were reminiscent of a Tokay. It is quite a delicate wine, less aromatic than those mentioned above and sometimes even a bit too neutral, but its lightness nevertheless makes it worthy of a place next to its prestigious cousins.

The Pinot Blanc (or Klevner) produces a supple, delicate and quite round wine which has, however, a rather timid and self-effacing personality, and so is often not very striking.

The Muscat has an even more penetrating fragrance than the Gewurztraminer; it is intense, almost to the point of being indiscreet. Its finesse suffers because of it but its aggressive smell attracts many followers. It is now a dry wine, but it used to be used in the production of sweet dessert wines.

The Sylvaner is honest, respectable and modest but with enough finesse, a reasonable acidity and a notable bouquet. However, it is not in the same class as a Riesling or a Gewurztraminer.

The Chasselas (or Gutedel) produces wonderful eating grapes, but the wine has little character, and only a faint aroma and hidden charm; it is not harsh but does not age well.

The Pinot Noir is grown little here. When it is, it produces a red wine similar to a Burgundy but, more importantly, a rosé, the *Clairet d'Alsace* or *Schillerwein* which is pale coloured, light bodied and has a good bouquet: it also has a good flavour and a certain verve which is not without its charm.

The *Alsace Edelzwicker* is a white wine that comes from a blend of various noble vines. Naturally enough its quality depends on the proportions of its components.

Alsace-Klevner de Heiligenstein (BAS-RHIN)
Benefits from its own *appellation*.

Alsace Grand Cru
This *appellation* is reserved for the higher quality wines from specifically designated sites that are sufficiently high in alcohol and accepted by a committee of experts.

The best villages are in Haut-Rhin. They include:

Ribeauvillé (Zahnacker and Trottacker *crus*)
Sigolsheim (Mamburg and Vogelgarten *crus*)
Kientzheim (Schlossberg *cru*)
Kaysersberg
Riquewihr
Mittelwihr
Zellenberg
Hunawihr
Westhalten
Beblenheim
Ammerschwihr (Kaefferkopf *cru*)
Turckheim (Brand *cru*)
Eguisheim.

Bas-Rhin also has a few *climats* that are worthy of interest:

Dambach
Kintzheim
Barr.

Crémant d'Alsace
A pleasant sparkling wine, made by the champagne method, that is light and very fruity; made from Riesling, Pinot Blanc, Pinot Noir, Pinot Gris or Chardonnay (Auxerrios) grapes.

Vins delimités de qualité supérieure

Côtes de Toul (MEURTHE-ET-MOSELLE)

On the border of the department of Meuse, this is a small vineyard planted with Pinot, Gamay and a few other vines that produces very little red or white wine, but quite a bit of a rosé wine called *Gris de Toul*. This wine is quite well liked for its vivaciousness, its incredible lightness, its pleasant gentleness and the fact that it ages well; however, its greenness can sometimes be aggressive.

Vins de Moselle

One or two villages scattered around the west of the department close to Metz produce rosé, red and a little white wine that is very light and quite cheeky but may be a little acidic.

Vins de consommation courante

These account for less than 10 per cent of the production of Alsace and are almost all white. Lorraine produces only a very small amount of very light reds and rosés that are often acidic.

19

JURA
THE ALPS

There are two mountain vineyards to the north and south of Lake Geneva that manage to survive despite the growing conditions that are much more difficult than on the hills or plains. The yield per hectare is low, and the work is labour-intensive. The price of the wine is therefore often higher, especially when the conditions for cultivating the vine are particularly difficult, as is the case in Arbois. The consumer is often put off by this.

GROWING CONDITIONS

In Jura the ground is limestone mixed with clay. The bedrock is marly. The alpine vineyards are found in the valleys and on the lower slopes, which are also mainly limestone.

The harsh climate restricts the choice of vines to indigenous varieties that are well adapted to the difficult conditions in this country of early winters and late springs, where frost is a dangerous enemy.

In Franche-Comté the white wines are made from the Savagnin grape (it is also called the Naturé), and from Chardonnay and Pinot Blanc; the reds are made from Poulsart, Trousseau and Pinot Noir.

In Savoie the white vines that are used the most are the Aligoté, the Roussette, the Chasselas and several indigenous varieties that give the small local *crus* their individuality; among the reds, Gamay, Mondeuse, Pinot and Persan dominate. Resistant hybrids are cultivated to make *vins de consommation courante*.

THE *CRUS*

Appellations d'origine contrôlées

Arbois (JURA)
This is the prestigious *appellation* of Franche-Comté. The fame of this vineyard is enhanced by the fact that it was here that Louis Pasteur began his series of experiments and discoveries on wine. The vineyard is dense but small, confined to the canton of Arbois.

Alsace: Winemakers working in the street
(Photograph by J. P. Verney – Ministry of Agriculture archives)

Rosé wines are produced in the largest quantities; they are light and lively wines that keep well; they have a delicate though not very intense aroma and a certain elegance; they develop an attractive bouquet.

Very few reds are produced.

The whites have similar qualities to the rosés, although each has its own special character taken from the vines peculiar to that region. 'Vin jaune' is a great curiosity, found only in Jura. It is a white wine made exclusively from Savagnin grapes. It is made in a similar way to Spanish sherry, although it only exists as a dry wine and never as a dessert wine. The process is based on growing a yeast mould on the surface of the wine. The wine is left in casks for at least six years without being filled up. Little is known about the changes that occur to bring about the hazelnut taste, known as the *grande jaune* because of the beautiful pale golden colour that appears. The loss of wine during the course of this long storage is considerable, and there are many failures, so that it is always a high priced wine. It is usually sold in the traditional bottle, the 'Clavelin'.

Another regional speciality is the *vin de paille* (straw wine). This is a dessert wine made by concentrating the grape juice by partially drying the grapes on a bed of straw before fermenting them. Nowadays it is extremely rare.

The commune of Pupillin may join its name to that of Arbois.

There is also an *Arbois mousseux*, a sparkling wine with a distinctive personality.

Château-Chalon (JURA)
This is made in four communes in the Voiteur region; their vineyards have excellent exposure to the sun and produce the best *vin jaune* – its flavour is particularly sharp but equally it is a wine of great finesse and calibre.

Côtes-du-Jura
These wines come from the whole of the southwest of the department, from a huge area of land that surrounds Lons-le-Saunier. Despite the vastness of the designated area, production is low. There are four times as many whites as reds. The whites vary a great deal in quality but are generally dry, light bodied and have a marked taste of the soil; they have a tendency to maderise.

L'Étoile (JURA)
A small group of three communes adjacent to Lons-le-Saumur producing white; yellow and sparkling wines. The name refers to the shape of the small fossil that is found in the soil of this region. The amounts produced commercially are very limited.

Vins de Savoie

These wines are produced mainly in the valleys of Savoie and Haute-Savoie that have the most sunshine. Their quality depends on where they were made and on the vine types. These are Gamay, Mondeuse, Pinot Noir, Persan and a few others for the reds and the rosés; Roussette (or Altesse), Chardonnay, Roussanne (or Bergeron) and Chasselas for the whites.

The red wines are often acidic and quite coarse, but the best ones do have a good aroma, and a few may age nicely. The whites are always lively, racy and amusing wines as long as they are not too acidic. They often have a certain finesse that gives them their charm.

There are a few *crus* that may add their name to the *appellation*: Les Abymes, Apremont, Arbin, Ayze, Charpignat, Chautagne, Chignin (or Chignin-Bergeron or Bergeron), Cruet, Marignan, Montmélian, Ripaille, Saint-Jean-de-la-Porte, Saint-Jeoire-Prieuré, Sainte-Marie-d'Alloix.

The volume of white wines produced is more than twice that of reds.

Roussette de Savoie or Vin de Savoie-Roussette
The Roussette, or Altesse grape, gives a lively and easy-going dry white wine of some distinction that has a seductive aroma. The following are worth noting: Frangy, Marestel (or Marestel-Altesse), Monterminod, Monthoux.

Vin de Savoie mousseux
A light sparkling wine that has an attractive liveliness about it. The wine from Ayze is judged to be especially good.

Seyssel
To the southwest of Geneva, sitting astride the departments of Ain and Haute-Savoie, this is a small vineyard comprising two communes that produces a white wine from the Roussette grape, a wine that deserves to be noticed for its characteristic flavour, its finesse and its balance.

Seyssel mousseux
Better known than the above, this is made from the Molette and Chasselas (the local Fendant) grapes; original and distinguished, with a delicate aroma.

Crépy
There are three communes situated on the hills of Crépy, to the south of Lake Geneva, where the cultivation of the Chasselas vine allows for the production of a dry white wine that has quite a particular flavour and is expansive, round and full, possessing a finesse that is both subtle and elegant.

(In some ways this is the French equivalent of the famous Fendant from the hills of the Swiss region of Lausanne on the opposite side of the river. However, it lacks the unusual exposure of the latter. Dezalay in Switzerland is in a unique position in that it faces south and receives the sun's rays as they bounce off the lake; it therefore gets a lot of sunshine and results in the production of fuller bodied and more expansive Fendant wines.)

Crépy wine retains a small amount of carbonation that produces a very pleasant light bubbliness when the wine is opened.

Vins delimités de qualité supérieure

Vin de Bugey and Roussette du Bugey
A large part of the department of Ain produces some reds and rosés of varying quality – they are often fruity, but quite light bodied. The following are worth mentioning: Virieu-le-Grand, Montagnieu, Manicle, Machuraz, Cerdon. The whites, made from the Roussette grape, are more interesting; they are fragrant and quite balanced. The following stand out: Anglefort, Arbignieu, Chanay, Lagnieu, Montagnieu, Virieu-le-Grand. Cerdon makes a *mousseux* (sparkling) and a *pétillant* (less sparkling) wine.

Vins de pays

Vin de pays des Balmes dauphinoises comes from a few cantons in Isere and Savoie.

Vin de pays d'Allobrogie is produced throughout the departments of Savoie and Haute-Savoie.

Vin de pays des coteaux du Grésivaudan comes from most of Isere and part of Savoie.

Vin de pays de Franche-Comté (Jura and Haute-Savoie).

Vins de consommation courante

These are mostly reds, the whites accounting for barely 10 per cent of production. They make up 90 per cent of the production of Franche-Comté and 50 per cent of the production of the Alps. They are mostly of local interest, and represent a minute proportion of the total French harvest (approximately 1 per cent).

20
SPIRITS

In France, spirits are known as *eaux-de-vie* (water that gives life), and Cognac, Armagnac, and many others are defined and protected by law. These include:

- *Eaux-de-vie de vin* (made from wine): de Bourgogne, des Côtes du Rhône, de la Marne, de Savoie, d'Aquitaine, du Bugey, du Centre-Est (Burgundy – Beaujolais – Champagne), des Coteaux de la Loire, de Franche-Comté, du Languedoc, de Provence, de Faugères.
- Fine Bordeaux is made in the same way as Cognac.
- *Eaux-de-vie de marc* (made from the fruit pulp): de Bourgogne, de Champagne, des Côtes du Rhône, d'Aquitaine, du Bugey, du Centre-Est, des Coteaux de la Loire, de Franche-Comté, du Languedoc, de Provence, de Savoie, d'Alsace-Gewurztraminer, d'Auvergne.
- *Eaux-de-vie de cidre* (made from cider): de Normandie, de Bretagne, du Maine.
- *Calvados*: du Pays d'Auge (the best known), du Calvados, du Cotentin, du Domfrontais, du Mortanais, du Pays de Bray, de l'Avranchin, de la Vallée de l'Orne, du Merlerault, du Pays de la Risle, du Perche.
- *Eaux-de-vie de poire* (made from pears): de Bretagne, de Maine, de Normandie. This is made by mashing up the fruit and distilling it. William pears give the best results.
- Mirabelle de Lorraine (yellow plums)

This may only come from certain districts of the departments of Meurthe-et-Moselle, Meuse, and Vosges.

Kirsch, which is made by distilling wild cherries, does not belong to the list of *eaux-de-vie* that are protected by an *appellation contrôlée*. The region around Fougerolles (Haute-Saône) is said to produce the best, but the ones from Alsace are equally remarkable.

Quetsch (blue plums) produce an *eau-de-vie de prune* which is not as delicate as the mirabelle.

Eau-de-vie de framboise (raspberry) is extremely aromatic. It is made by infusing the fruit in alcohol, which is then distilled. If kept for too long it loses its beautiful fragrance. The best *eaux-de-vie* are made from the wild raspberries of Alsace.